Praise for

On the Frontline

"No tactical field manual will help you when the bullets are flying if you don't have your head on straight, and that is where *On the Frontline* comes in. Read it. Take it to heart. You'll be glad you did."

    —CHUCK HOLTON, author, army ranger, and CBN
      adventure correspondent

"God's word and *On the Frontline* are a must in order to lead a complete and victorious life as a Christian warrior. Don't deploy without Tom Neven's operational manual on Christian living in the military!"

    —LT. GENERAL BRUCE L. FISTER, USAF (RETIRED),
      executive director of Officers' Christian Fellowship
      of the USA

"Tom Neven offers clear and concise answers to the questions and concerns that plague military members and their families. This book needs to be on every frontline reading list of military members from every branch of the service."

    —ELLIE KAY, best-selling author of *Heroes at Home* and
      keynote speaker for the Heroes at Home World Tour

"If you're looking for God's answers to man's dilemmas, this book is a great tool—particularly for the men and women on America's frontlines."

> —COLONEL JEFF O'LEARY, USAF (RETIRED), FOX News
> military analyst

"Tom Neven steels the heart and soul for the warfare, both worldly and spiritual, that awaits the warrior. Neven speaks with the wisdom and authority of a scout who has walked the trail and knows how to get to the objective without falling prey to the enemy."

> —LT. COLONEL GARY WALSH, U.S. ARMY (RETIRED),
> infantry and legal officer who served combat tours in
> Grenada and Somalia

★★★★

On the Frontline

Foreword by General Charles C. Krulak,
31st Commandant of the Marine Corps
★★★★

On the Frontline

A Personal Guidebook for the Physical, Emotional, and Spiritual Challenges of Military Life

TOM NEVEN

WATERBROOK
PRESS

On the Frontline
Published by WaterBrook Press
12265 Oracle Boulevard, Suite 200
Colorado Springs, Colorado 80921
A division of Random House Inc.

10-Digit ISBN: 1-4000-7335-9
13-Digit ISBN: 978-1-4000-7335-1

Library of Congress Cataloging-in-Publication Data
Neven, Tom, 1956-
   On the frontline : a personal guidebook for the physical, emotional, and spiritual challenges of military life / Tom Neven. — 1st ed.
      p. cm.
   Includes bibliographical references.
   ISBN-13: 978-1-4000-7335-1
   ISBN-10: 1-4000-7335-9
   1. Soldiers—Religious life. 2. Christian life. I. Title.
   BV4588.N48 2006
   248.8'8—dc22

                                    2006026644

Printed in the United States of America
2006—First Edition

10 9 8 7 6 5 4 3 2 1

SPECIAL SALES
Most WaterBrook books are available in special quantity discounts when purchased in bulk by corporations, organizations and special interest groups. Custom imprinting or excerpting can also be done to fit special needs. For information, please e-mail SpecialMarkets@WaterBrookPress.com or call 1-800-603-7051.

★★★★

To my son, Joshua, lover of all things military,
who had the great foresight to be born on the
Marine Corps birthday, November 10.
And to my wife, Colette, and daughter, Hannah,
thanks for your patience as I worked on this project.

Contents

Acknowledgments xi

Foreword xiii

1   The Power of Discipline 1

2   God's Faithfulness on the Frontline 27

3   The Mental Burdens of Military Life 49

4   Getting the Most from Teamwork 73

5   Taking Control of Your Finances 95

6   God's Rules for Great Sex 113

7   Protecting the Home Front 133

8   What to Do with Your Anger 151

9   Getting Answers About Grief 169

10   Finding God on the Frontline 189

Notes 207

Acknowledgments

I received tremendous help in researching this book from many members of the U.S. military, both past and present. I would like to thank in particular Lieutenant Commander Steve Sauders, First Lieutenant Adam Morehouse, Staff Sergeant Toph Bailey, Sergeant Les Shaw, Colonel Paul Meredith, Captain Luke Haverstick, First Lieutenant Blake Smith, Captain Krista Jekielek, John Thurman, and Tom Iannucci for their invaluable contributions. Thanks also to Chuck Milligan, Chuck Holton ("Let's go exploring!"), Leon Lowman, and Ellie and Bob Kay for their help and friendship.

Foreword

Therefore take up the whole armor of God,
that you may be able to withstand in the evil
day, and having done all, to stand. Stand therefore, having girded your waist with the truth,
having put on the breastplate of righteousness,
and having shod your feet with the preparation
of the gospel of peace; above all, taking the
shield of faith with which you will be able to
quench all the fiery darts of the wicked one.
And take the helmet of salvation, and the
sword of the Spirit, which is the word of God.

EPHESIANS 6:13-17, NKJV

Service in our armed forces demands a depth of character. Men
and women who can reach deep within themselves and draw upon
an inner strength, borne of faith, have always carried the day
against those of lesser character. When the battlefield is chaotic and

horror is all about, it is those who have taken care to build their character who emerge victorious.

Cowardliness in one's character will sooner or later manifest itself in other forms of cowardliness. Those who have the courage to face up to the ethical challenges in their daily lives will find that same courage can be drawn upon in times of great stress and in times of battle.

So, who are you really? What do you stand for? What is the essence of your character?

Every day we make decisions. Every day presents each of us with a prescribed amount of time and new circumstances and choices. How we fill that time and how we deal with those circumstances and choices are key to our character development. Quite simply, we are the ones who define who we are and who we will be. We choose our character, we develop our character, and we build our character by making right choices. Integrity, trustworthiness, selflessness, loyalty, and dependability all help provide a firm foundation.

For Christians, the cornerstone to the foundation of character is faith. As Paul said to the Ephesians, "above all, taking the shield of faith with which you will be able to quench all the fiery darts of the wicked one" (Ephesians 6:16, NKJV). Living your faith will strengthen the decision-making process and lead to right decisions when you are faced with tough choices.

As you serve your nation, support for your faith will come

from many sources. One such source is Tom Neven's book *On the Frontline*. I encourage you to read and re-read this book. It provides biblical wisdom, help, hope, and encouragement for your day-to-day life in service to God and country.

—General Charles C. Krulak, USMC (retired)

31st Commandant of the Marine Corps

★★★★

On the Frontline

1

★★★★

The Power of Discipline

The Best Training Comes Through Hardship

Let us run with perseverance the
race marked out for us.

HEBREWS 12:1

C hallenge. The word could be synonymous with "military." In fact, you probably entered the military welcoming the challenge, seeking to test yourself against the best. You wanted to prove you have what it takes, and you *did* prove it. You earned a place in the United States military, the most powerful fighting force known to man.

You have gained hard-won experience, and you're making your mark in the military. But, of course, the demands don't get any lighter. There is no other profession as pressure packed as serving in the armed forces. Some days you love it, I know. And some days you probably ask yourself why you chose this career path.

The good news is that God has you where you are for a reason, and he wants to use you in a way that will amaze even yourself. The pressure and hardship might seem overwhelming at times, but you serve a limitless God. And not only that, you number among the most disciplined and the most highly trained warriors on the planet. Obedience and discipline are keys to success in the military, just as they are in the Christian life and life in general. The lessons you are learning will serve you well for the rest of your life.

In Iraq, our military is battling not only the insurgency but also the incredible, stifling heat. It fills the air and radiates from the ground. If you don't stay hydrated, you can die. First Lieutenant Adam Morehouse, an artillery officer by training, is all too familiar with the deadly desert heat. It can become almost a living thing that crushes the breath out of men and women conducting missions in Iraq. And the demands are mental as well as physical—the pressure can be overwhelming.

Morehouse describes a battalion-sized cordon-and-search mission in a neighborhood near Baghdad, conducted by the Second Infantry Division. His job was to take a team of soldiers and block off one of the highways into town. They were going to be sitting along a road, out in the open, for as long as ten hours. Long before the mission was to start, Morehouse racked his sleep-deprived brain: *Does everyone know his job? Do we have everything we need? Will we get hit?*

He collapsed onto his cot, trying to get some rest. His fear was intense. He prayed to God, asking for wisdom and peace. Finally, he drifted off to sleep.

"After I woke up," he said, "I felt almost a day-and-night change. I felt a complete sense of peace. I'd done everything I could. We were in God's hands."

The mission went off without a hitch and without anyone getting hurt. Recently, Morehouse looked back at that experience. "It was the most tangible time in my life that God had directly, instantly, quickly answered a prayer in an obvious way," he said.

Without his faith in God, Lieutenant Morehouse is not sure how he could have handled the pressure. "At every stage of your life you have to make a fresh decision to obey him," he said. "You can't make just one decision and coast on it for the rest of your life. You have to decide every day to be obedient to the Lord and work hard at it. I believe God has me in the Army for a reason, and I trust that he's still taking care of me. You have to continually seek God's face."

STANDING UP UNDER PRESSURE

The pressure begins the moment you enter basic training. In fact, you feel the force of it as soon as you step off the bus.

In my case, it was late, nearly midnight. I'd spent the past five hours on a Greyhound bus traveling from Jacksonville, Florida. We had a short layover in Savannah, Georgia, before pulling out of the bus station, over the towering Savannah bridge and into the night, headed into the South Carolina lowlands. I had only a vague idea of what lay ahead, even though I had volunteered for it.

I sat by myself in the dark, watching trees that dripped Spanish moss flash by in the bus's headlights. As we wound through the back roads, riffs from that summer's Top 40 hit "Love Will Keep Us Together" kept playing in my mind, crowding out thoughts or doubts before they formed. I didn't want to think about why I was riding this bus or whether this was what I really wanted to be doing.

There were occasional mileage signs along the way: Hilton Head, 25 miles; Hardeeville, 10 miles; but there were no signs for where we were going.

About an hour after the bus left Savannah, we rounded a curve and there it was. A sentry booth guarded the entrance to a long causeway where a large red sign with gold lettering read: Marine Corps Recruit Depot, Parris Island, South Carolina.

I had arrived.

The driver stopped on the curve and opened the bus's door with a hiss of escaping air. I joined five other young men getting off the bus, as the passengers bound for Beaufort and points beyond busied themselves with newspapers or buried their faces deeper into makeshift pillows. At the door we were greeted by a puff of warm, humid air that smelled of swamp. We headed toward the sentry booth, where a Marine in blue trousers, khaki shirt, and white garrison cap stood, hands on hips, awaiting our arrival.

We sauntered across the road, joking in subdued voices.

"GET OVER HERE—NOW!" he roared.

His voice shook me. The muscles of my legs and buttocks reacted almost involuntarily, as if jolted by a cattle prod. I ran to the gate.

"GET IN LINE! STAND AT ATTENTION!"

We ran to the curb the sentry pointed to, and I fell in at the end of the line. Assuming my best high-school-marching-band position of attention, I remembered not to lock my knees. The sentry didn't seem to know what to do with us; this apparently was not the usual way for recruits to arrive. They normally came in a full bus and were driven to the receiving barracks on base. He made a phone call, constantly looking toward us as if we were going to run away. He concluded the conversation. "Okay, they'll be waiting for you."

The sentry turned to us, his voice only a few decibels lower than when he previously addressed us. "Stand there. A van will be out to pick you up."

So we stood there in the humid South Carolina night. Meanwhile, cars full of Marines returning from liberty entered the gate. We were pelted with laughs, jeers, you'll be sorrys. We must have looked ridiculous, standing there at awkward attention in our civilian clothes and long hair.

I was disoriented and a bit afraid. I realized later that this was nothing more than the age-old tradition of hazing new members of an elite organization. It was an affirmation of pride; we were the outsiders who had not yet proven our worthiness to belong to *their* Marine Corps.

Soon a van approached the sentry booth, and an avuncular black man in civilian clothing got out and spoke with the sentry. We were told to climb into the van, and I immediately felt a sense of impending judgment. What had I gotten myself into? The driver only added to my confusion. After the gruffness of the sentry, he was friendly and talkative. As we drove down a long causeway lined with palmetto and neatly trimmed shrubbery, he told us that if we had any weapons, particularly knives, we should throw them out the window now before we got to the receiving barracks.

On the island, we drove past maintenance buildings and then barracks. Huge steam pipes lined the road, snaking and curving over and around obstacles. On the left was a paved drill field, empty this time of night. The only illumination came from street-lights and stairwell lights in the barracks.

We made a right turn, then a left, and stopped outside a two-story white clapboard building. I recognized the sign over the doorway: "Through this portal pass prospects for the world's finest fighting force." It struck me as being in the same vein as Dante's counsel: "All hope abandon, ye who enter here."

A man in a Smokey Bear hat waited, hands on hips, as the van pulled up. Before one of the other new arrivals could open the van's door, this man—a drill instructor, otherwise known as a DI—barked out a Neanderthal sound. I don't know what he yelled. The mere fact that we were the objects of his wrath jerked us into motion. We tumbled out of the van.

"GET ON THE YELLOW HOOF PRINTS! YOU BETTER HURRY UP."

I saw a formation of yellow footprints painted on the pavement, but due to my fright or naiveté I looked for yellow horseshoe prints. I finally figured out what he wanted and jumped on the first pair of footprints I saw. I was first in line, so I could see into the door of the barracks. Many other men in civilian clothes, recruits who had arrived earlier that evening, for some reason stood at rigid attention next to tables with silver tops. The DI came up behind me, bending close to my ear.

"Do you see that private in there?" he asked in a menacing voice. The hair stood up on the back of my neck. I didn't see any private. I couldn't see anyone in uniform. I hadn't yet caught on that we were all privates, and the one in question was the man standing closest to the open door. Still, I nodded.

"I want you to go in there and stand at attention next to him," the DI said. I nodded again, and he grunted out a loud, "MOVE!" I jumped a few inches in the air, as if in a Tex Avery cartoon, and ran up the few steps and into the brightly lit room. Taking a chance, I stopped next to the first man, the private in question.

The long room was full of other men standing at attention.

Some already had their heads shaved, although they still wore civilian clothes. A large desk such as you might find in a police station dominated the middle of the room, and several uniformed Marines lounged around it. On the walls of the room were red wooden signs with yellow lettering:

"The first and last word out of your mouth will always be 'Sir!'"

"If you want to use the rest room, you will ask the drill instructor: 'Sir, Private _____ requests permission to use the head, sir!'"

"You will respond to all orders by sounding off 'Aye aye, sir!'"

The Marines' recruiting slogan offers no compromise: "We Don't Promise You a Rose Garden."

WHAT ARE YOU AFTER?

For me, this was the culmination of a dream. Okay, it was the *beginning* of the culmination. One of my earliest memories is as a first-grader sitting at my desk at Hoover Elementary School in Crawfordsville, Indiana, daydreaming about being the youngest member of the Marine Corps, riding to school in the back of a Jeep while wearing the Corps' Dress Blue uniform, chauffeured by two adult Marines wearing their own snappy Dress Blues. Shortly after that my family moved to Florida, and I played Marine in the surf at the beach, fantasizing amphibious assaults on the sands of the Sunshine State. As a teenager, I devoured books on military history and strategy.

Still, enlisting in the military was not the popular thing to do at the time. America's involvement in the Vietnam War had officially ended two years earlier, but the situation that spring of 1975 was far from peaceful, and there was fear the United States could be dragged back into the war. Ironically, on the day I signed the dotted line—March 10, 1975—North Vietnam launched a final offensive that would culminate in the fall of South Vietnam in less than two months. My high school friends just couldn't understand my decision. Why the Marines?

On the surface, a life of rigorous discipline and obedience doesn't look all that appealing. Some of the strongest natural tendencies inside us rebel at the thought. And at the time I couldn't put into words why I wanted to join the military. As I look back, though, I realize I wanted to be part of something larger than myself, I wanted adventure, and I wanted to be challenged.

My friend Chuck Holton, a former Army Ranger, was much more articulate about his yearnings as a fifteen-year-old. He wrote in his journal:

There's so much that I haven't done that I want to do. So many things I haven't seen, been to, experienced. I'm anxious and excited! What's God got for me? It's like I'm standing on the edge of an ocean of possibilities. I can't see the other side, but I know it's great. I can't wait to cross, and I know that although there will always be the peaks

and the troughs, every step is an adventure. Life is LIFE!
Fill me to overflowing.[1]

Holton had a big advantage over me because he knew God. I did not. But in my case, God was using the Marines as a first step in bringing me to himself.

I recognize now that, deep down, my desire to become a Marine was a desire for significance. I needed to do something that mattered. Everyone has a yearning for something bigger than himself. It has been described as the God-shaped hole that we all seek to fill in some way. In his *Confessions,* Saint Augustine wrote of God, "You have made us for yourself, and our heart is restless until it rests in you."[2] Sometimes, though, filling the restless void can be a lot harder than we imagine. Sometimes God takes us through a wilderness experience to teach us something important. One big reason why is that sometimes the lesson won't stick any other way.

LEARNING DISCIPLINE IN THE WILDERNESS

Moses had to wander on the back side of the desert for forty years before he was prepared for God to use him to confront Pharaoh and lead the Hebrews to freedom. Later in the history of Israel, God chose a shepherd boy, David, to be king of Israel. But David first had to spend months in the wilderness, running from his enemy, Saul, before he was ready to assume the throne. Various

Old Testament prophets also had to endure tough times as part of fulfilling God's purposes. Even Jesus spent forty days fasting in the Judean desert at the beginning of his ministry.

Basic training, in its own way, is like being trained in the wilderness. The process takes us outside ourselves and makes us think in ways we haven't had to before. It breaks us down so that the military can mold us into men and women who can fulfill a mission. It trains us to be sensitive to orders and to understand the importance of obedience. The biblical figures who were trained by God in the wilderness learned these same lessons.

Knowing in the abstract that boot camp will be tough and coming face to face with a tough DI are two entirely different things. I was standing in a room full of frightened recruits being stalked by madmen wearing funny hats. It was late and the heat was sweltering, even at night. Never mind my lifelong dream to be a Marine—I wanted to be anywhere but there.

The early days of boot camp, called First Phase, were the hardest. But slowly, gradually, I toughened both physically and mentally. The physical training became a little easier. I was also getting more accustomed to the DIs' constant demands and the instant obedience they required.

The Power of Individual Discipline

In addition to learning to function as a team in the Marines, we had myriad individual skills to master. Some things we could do only by ourselves, such as fighting with the pugil stick. This training weapon was used to simulate close combat with a rifle. Each stick—pole, really—was about five feet long with large padded ends. In theory, each fight would consist of elegant thrusts and parries, with a clean blow to the head, neck, or upper torso counting as a kill. In reality, the matches quickly degenerated into wild swinging, staggering, and, usually, at least one person flat on his back.

During our platoon's first session with pugil sticks, I was on one of my periodic spells of light duty for tendonitis. While I was out of commission, the other recruits were shown several tricks for fighting. When we revisited the pugil sticks in Third Phase, all the other recruits had the benefit of at least some experience. I was a rookie. And adding to my sense of dread, the DIs introduced a new wrinkle to the fights: two against one.

We marched as a four-platoon series to the sandy pugil stick pits, where each platoon formed a side of the square. The platoon sat in the grass alongside the pit as instructors conducted quick refresher training, and then it was time to start. The DIs encouraged us to cheer for fellow platoon members, and the scene soon took on the air of a gladiatorial contest.

I was genuinely scared as I awaited my turn. After a few fights—my platoon was losing more than it was winning—one of our DIs, Staff Sergeant Pulley, looked over our platoon. I looked down, as if lack of eye contact would somehow make me invisible. Still, his eyes settled on me. I, who had absolutely no experience with a pugil stick, was chosen to face two opponents. Weak at the knees and with gargantuan butterflies in my belly, I went to get suited up.

As I strapped on the heavy gloves, padded groin protector, and the football helmet with mesh face mask, I was sure I was done for. My heart pounded in my throat as I grasped the pugil stick; it was much heavier than I'd expected. I ventured into the center of the pit, where the referee told me to hold my spot. My two opponents seemed to tower over me. They were ready to put me in a world of hurt.

The referee blew the whistle for the match to start, and a passing comment he'd made in the refresher course flashed into my mind: when fighting two or more opponents, keep moving so they can't come at you two-abreast. That way, one would always be blocked by his partner. I began a rapid sidestep and tried my best to remember the jabs and swings we'd been taught in our close-combat training with the rifle.

The sand seemed to grab my feet and hold them, slowing me down. Blows rained down on my arms and shoulders; fortunately none counted as a kill. The fight became a blur of colors and pain, grunts and curses. The rest of the world vanished as I tried desperately to fend off the blows and to make my own feeble counterattack. The stick became heavier, and I soon felt as if I were flailing uselessly. My shoulder muscles burned, my lungs gasped for air, and my legs were turning to jelly as I danced around my opponents in the sand.

Suddenly, the referee's whistle blew. He motioned to one of my opponents with a slashing motion to the neck, meaning the recruit had been killed. I looked at the referee in disbelief as a roar went up from my platoon. *I'd done that?* Pure luck, no doubt.

Still, I faced a remaining foe. My arms were growing weaker, my jabs and swings more ineffectual. But my adversary seemed to have slowed even more. He was also looking a bit worried. I was ready to end this thing—NOW! I was seized by a new aggressiveness, and whereas my first kill was probably luck, I found myself aiming a direct slashing blow to his head. My first shot missed, but I was driving him back with a flurry of blows and jabs. Suddenly, the whistle blew again. The referee motioned toward my opponent's head—he was out.

I triumphantly raised the pugil stick over my head in a scene straight out of *Gladiator*. My platoon roared its approval. "Nice job, recruit," the referee said as he helped me strip off the protective gear, and that compliment stoked a fire in my chest. For the first time since arriving at Parris Island, I had a sense of having done something truly significant. Later, in the barracks, I realized my thumb had been seriously smashed despite the protective gloves. I hadn't felt it during the fight or in the period following. As I stood examining my throbbing digit, lost in thought, Pulley's voice came from the front of the squad bay.

"If you can move it, it's not broken."

I looked up, surprised. He had a slight smile on his face; I sensed he was proud of me. I also sensed he had not expected such an outcome when he chose me, considering I was not the most studly recruit in the platoon. (I'm six-one now, but the last four of those inches came in a final growth spurt *after* boot camp.) Maybe when he sent me into the sand pit he sensed I was capable of more. I'll never know.

Following God in the Military

Looking back, I realize it doesn't matter what was behind the DI's decision to send me up against two armed opponents. Serving in uniform means you will be asked to do things you're sure you are not capable of. And then, after plunging in, you find that you are capable of much more than you thought. As someone has said, "God does not call the qualified; he qualifies the called."

It's a good thing God is involved in our training, because without his help in overcoming our lower nature we'd be hard pressed to develop the discipline and obedience necessary to succeed in the military. As you well know, these are two of the hardest things in life to master, and it's not because of laziness or a secret desire to fail. It's because we are born with a sin nature that automatically rebels whenever we are told what to do by a higher authority (see Genesis 3:1, 4, 6). Human nature is referred to in the New Testament as the "old self" (see Colossians 3:9).

Our original nature, which remains active even after we become Christians, wars against our new nature, given to us by Christ (see 2 Corinthians 5:17; Romans 7:15–25). The conflict between the two comes out in everyday life, whether you're a civilian or in uniform. But in the pressure cooker of military life, you could rightly say the war between our old nature and our new nature assumes biblical proportions. Living up to the expectations of our DIs in boot camp was hard. Living up to the life God calls us to is much harder.

Thankfully, we're not alone in this struggle. Think about the task set before Moses. God called him to take on the most powerful man in the world, the pharaoh of Egypt, and to demand that Pharaoh free the Hebrew slaves. Moses was, quite understandably, afraid. He was also uncertain of his own abilities. In fact, he made sure God was aware of his many deficiencies. "Moses said to the LORD, 'O Lord, I have never been eloquent, neither in the past nor since you have spoken to your servant. I am slow of speech and tongue'" (Exodus 4:10). But God would have none of it. "The LORD said to him, 'Who gave man his mouth? Who makes him deaf or mute? Who gives him sight or makes him blind? Is it not I, the LORD? Now go; I will help you speak and will teach you what to say'" (Exodus 4:11–12).

Unlike the ancient warriors of God, we will not stand face to face in opposition to the world's most powerful king, as Moses did, or face a giant, as the boy David did. Instead, in light of today's wars, you might face insurgents who easily blend into the crowd. Every pothole in the road and every piece of trash might be a vehicle-destroying bomb. You might be caught in the middle of warring factions, countrymen who can't seem to settle their differences without resorting to arms.

In fulfilling your mission, you might also have to fight discouragement. What will it take to bring about good in a land that seems intent on thwarting all attempts to restore peace and order? If you are serving in Iraq or Afghanistan, you are putting your life on the line to help a country in turmoil, and the solutions are far from simple.

You know already that in the military, the pressure doesn't let up. The demands are constant and often seem to require superhuman strength and wisdom. And in a sense, they *do* require that level of strength and wisdom. It's a good thing you have God as a guide. Just as God directed David, Moses, and other warriors in ancient times, he stands ready to help you today.

Colonel Paul Meredith, who recently retired after twenty-seven years in the Army, stressed that you cannot be passive in seeking God's help. "You have to be proactive to nurture your faith," he said. "Soldiers have a lot of discretionary time. You have to choose to build a discipleship group, to seek an accountability partner, to find the chaplain and let him know who you are and that you're a believer.

"Always get involved in a prayer group," he added. "These have been the best, the closest relationships I ever had in the Army. Those are the guys who are your closest friends. They're the ones who'll pray for you, care for you. I don't see how anyone can sustain a real spiritual life if you don't build those things in."

★★★★

In this book we will take a realistic look at the struggles that confront men and women in uniform. We'll discuss anger, fear, depression, grief, and sexual temptation. We also will examine the day-to-day challenges you face—managing your finances, maximizing teamwork, keeping your most important relationships strong, dealing with loneliness, and maintaining your marriage from long distance. In every instance, we will focus on resources and solutions that are available to every member of the military—to help you succeed physically, emotionally, and spiritually.

★★★★

Life Practices That Enhance Your Success

Pressure, stress, and constant demands are part and parcel of military life. What are the practical steps you can take that will help you stand up under the burdens you carry as a member of the armed forces?

1. Realize that God is with you in the midst of pressure. The pressure will eat you alive if you let it, and a stressed-out soldier is a less-than-effective soldier. One key truth to keep in mind is that God is with you, even in the most demanding assignments. God is there, and his presence can produce a sense of control and a clear-headedness that might otherwise elude you.

   Pick a time when you are *not* under extreme pressure and familiarize yourself with stories of God's presence with others who operated in high-stress situations. God sent his angel into the furnace of fire to protect Shadrach, Meshach, and Abednego, who had remained faithful to God in defiance of the king's order to worship an idol (see Daniel 3:13–30). God protected David when he and his troops were being hunted by

David's son Absalom and his soldiers, who were trying to kill David (see 2 Samuel 15–18; Psalm 3). Likewise, when King Saul was seeking to kill David, God was near and heard David's prayers (see 1 Samuel 18:9–12, 29; Psalm 57).

2. Remember that it's not all up to you. Your involvement is crucial to the success of an operation, but your performance is not the *only* determinant of a positive outcome. You are part of a team. Focus on your max performance, and you will be doing all you can to assure a successful mission. Success comes from working together as a team, not as individuals.

3. Don't forget that you control only one thing. Part of the fruit of God's Spirit, available to every believer, is self-control (see Galatians 5:22–23). God controls the universe, and he allows you to exercise control over one thing: yourself. You can control your performance by operating at your full potential. But you can't control the outcome. Don't put that kind of pressure on yourself.

4. Take advantage of healthy stress-relievers. Alcohol and drugs, escapist fantasy and illicit sex, or other destructive outlets might appear to be effective stress-relievers. But any relief they offer will only be temporary, and in the end they create far more problems than they promise to solve. Avoid the lure of artificial escapes and instead make use of healthy stress-relievers. Every base has a club where you'll

be tempted to relieve stress through alcohol. But every base also has a gym, a pool, and other recreational facilities. Exercise, sports, pursuing a hobby, taking a course in a subject that interests you, service projects, and other such venues provide ways to express your creativity and talent, ways to explore outside interests, and ways to invest your abilities in helping others. A change of pace and outside diversions do a lot to help when you're constantly under the gun. Take advantage of opportunities offered by the USO and other service organizations.

5. Draw on the power of two. Identify a close friend who can serve as your confidant. Blow off steam, vent, tell him what pushes you to your limit. A good friend will be a good listener; even if he can't solve a particular problem himself, the value of having someone listen and offer support is immeasurable. And when you're asked to offer this type of trustworthy friendship, do the same for your friend.

6. Find the things that inspire you to obedience. Since obeying authority does not come naturally to any of us, it's useful to gain inspiration from real-life stories. Study the stories of biblical characters who remained obedient to God, to duty, and to what is right in spite of overwhelming opposition. For starters, read the book of Job; the account of Jesus in the Garden of Gethsemane (see

Matthew 26:36–44); and the stoning of Stephen (see Acts 6:8–7:1; 7:54–60). And remember, part of obeying God is obeying those appointed over you. "Obey your leaders and submit to their authority. They keep watch over you as men who must give an account. Obey them so that their work will be a joy, not a burden, for that would be of no advantage to you" (Hebrews 13:17).

7. Acknowledge to God that on your own, you are not equal to the challenge. Most of your days are crammed with incredible demands and daunting responsibilities that would turn the average person into a blubbering fool. And face it: On your own you're not equal to the task. But God is. God calls you to perform extraordinary feats, often in areas in which you are convinced you will fail. But God knows better. In fact, God delights in confounding the world by calling the least likely of heroes to perform amazing feats (see 1 Samuel 17:20–51; Exodus 3:1, 7–12). "But God chose the foolish things of the world to shame the wise; God chose the weak things of the world to shame the strong" (1 Corinthians 1:27).

God is looking for your willingness to obey, not how impressive you are on the outside. David, the warrior king of Israel, was known as a man after God's own heart (see 1 Samuel 13:14). Further, when God chose the shepherd boy David to be the second king of Israel, he passed over

David's older, stronger, more physically impressive brothers. "The LORD does not look at the things man looks at. Man looks at the outward appearance, but the LORD looks at the heart" (1 Samuel 16:7). Tell God that you realize you're not equal to the task but that you also know he is *more* than equal. With God, all things are possible (see Matthew 19:26).

2

God's Faithfulness on the Frontline

The Lord's Promises Are Greater Than Our Fear

The LORD himself goes before you and
will be with you; he will never leave you
nor forsake you. Do not be afraid;
do not be discouraged.

DEUTERONOMY 31:8

S erving in the armed forces is one of the few occupations that guarantees regular opportunities for sustaining serious injury and even death. Police officers and firefighters are acquainted with the same dangers, but in the military you face enemies who are *committed* to your destruction. This knowledge weighs on your mind—there is no escaping it.

After serving in Iraq, Staff Sergeant Toph Bailey of the Oregon National Guard knows what it's like to be in a tight spot. His convoy of trucks had already been under attack on the night they were moving outside Najaf. Suddenly Bailey and his troops drove into another ambush—this one almost a kilometer long.

"There must have been nearly four hundred, or [even] five hundred, enemy fighters lined up on both sides of the road," he recalled. "We had already been ambushed five times that night and had to keep driving back and forth on the main supply route in order to keep it open. I was in the trail vehicle when I saw a wall of tracers from both sides of the road suddenly form in front of us."

Over the roar of continuous fire, Bailey could hear bullets ricocheting off his truck's armor. Other rounds made whip-crack sounds as bullets snapped past his head. Suddenly a huge bang and flash struck the side of his truck—a rocket-propelled grenade (RPG) round! The vehicle rocked to the left and filled with smoke.

"It burned our eyes and we couldn't breathe," he said. "I thought for sure we were a 'mobility kill' and the enemy was going to overwhelm our truck, pull us out, and drag us around as they tore our bodies apart."

The Americans decided to push the convoy through the ambush. It seemed an RPG was whizzing by every second. The enemy also had placed an improvised explosive device (IED) along the ambush route, but that, too, failed to stop the trucks.

"It must have been disheartening for them, considering the size and volume of the ambush," Bailey said. Even with up to five hundred fighters, "they couldn't stop a single truck. That said, the vehicles could hardly drive and barely made it inside the wire six miles south."

After fighting through several ambushes in one night, Bailey was thankful to be alive. But as he now reflects on the ordeal, he says the danger didn't open his eyes to God's presence, as some might expect.

"I have to be honest; I never felt that [God's nearness], at least not the way most Christians think I would," he said. "People seem to look for a particular traumatic event or experience that I went through where I was protected by an invisible shield or something of that nature." Bailey said those who hear about his wartime experiences might expect that he would have fallen on his knees "weeping and repenting" after God got him through a particularly harrowing mission.

"This never happened," he said simply.

Instead, Bailey said, in addition to his military training and his prayers for wisdom, he relied on a basic faith in God. "I approached every day and every circumstance pretty much the same: 'If I die today, then that is God's will, and there is nothing I can do about it. I'm in his hands.' I concentrated on my mission and my men. I think that is what God expected of me."

GOD HOLDS YOUR LIFE

Toph Bailey's battle-tested wisdom and trust can benefit all of us. If you are serving in Iraq or Afghanistan, you literally live in the presence of your enemies. And if you are stationed away from the war zones, there are still daily reminders that you have chosen a career that puts you in harm's way. Serving in the military is not for the fainthearted.

In 1980, I was part of the Marine detachment at the U.S. Mission to the United Nations in Geneva, Switzerland. (The Marine Corps provides guards to embassies and other overseas diplomatic facilities.) As the assistant noncommissioned officer in charge—called the A/NCOIC, or, more simply, the A-slash—I supervised the Marines manning the two posts in the Mission building itself and two posts in a building about a mile away where the Strategic Arms Limitation Talks with the Soviet Union were being held.

I was standing with the Marine on duty in Post One, situated in the basement of the Mission with a bulletproof window that looked out into the parking garage. It was the operational center for the building, with a bank of sensors and cameras that kept an eye on the entire compound. The Marine on Post One controlled the complex; he could stop elevators in midfloor, he controlled all building entrances, and, most important, he controlled the front gate. On one of the electrical panels was a big red button. Hitting it would summon police and military personnel from every Swiss agency responsible for diplomatic security.

Should the Mission come under attack, we were told to hit the button before we did anything else. This was important because an attack or act of sabotage was a very real possibility. At that time a number of Americans were being held hostage at the

American Embassy in Teheran, Iran, and about a year earlier mobs had attacked the embassy in Islamabad, Pakistan, killing one of the Marines.

But the red button came with a caveat. If we hit it and it turned out to be a false alarm, the Swiss would supposedly charge the United States $10,000 for the effort, and if it was determined that the Marine had done so negligently, the big bucks would come out of his pocket. I don't think that was literally true, but we all believed it at the time, and that made us extremely reluctant to push the red button.

With that at the back of my mind, I watched a Post One monitor that showed a man on a motorcycle pull into the shadow of a tree across the street from the Mission's front gate. He was dressed in motorcycle leathers, and a dark visor on his helmet obscured his face. He sat on his motorcycle, staring at the gate, partially hidden in the shade. At about the same time, the ambassador's driver pulled his car into the garage next to Post One. He opened the car's back door in anticipation of the ambassador's departure.

I couldn't let the ambassador drive through the gate without finding out who was waiting in the shade. For a moment I contemplated the red button, but I had nothing more than suspicion to go on. It was just one man on a motorcycle. I told the Marine on duty, "Don't let the ambassador leave until I come back. And *don't* open the front gate!"

Never mind that I didn't have the authority to tell the ambassador what to do. As I headed across the parking lot toward the gate, I unfastened the leather stay on the holster holding the .38 caliber revolver on my hip. (The military sidearm at the time was still the .45 caliber pistol, but the State Department insisted that Marines carry the smaller caliber weapon, probably because it was more "diplomatic.") I approached the gate, and motorcycle man didn't budge. I have to admit I was afraid.

As I walked up to the steel barrier, motorcycle man moved toward me. My right arm tensed toward my pistol. He stopped, took off his helmet, and waved to me. He was the boyfriend of one of the nationals who worked as a secretary at the Mission. I'd seen him around, particularly at the TGIF parties we threw at the Marine House. In his halting English he tried to explain that he was waiting to pick up his girlfriend.

I told him he couldn't park his motorcycle there and would have to find someplace else to wait. He agreed to move to the corner of the block, away from the gate. I waved good-bye, headed back toward the building—and heaved a huge sigh of relief.

FACING THE PROSPECT OF DEATH

Sure, I had been scared, and for a moment my heart jumped into my throat when he first moved toward me. But I also realized another thing: Fear and dread are not the same thing. Fear in a dangerous situation is normal, even healthy. It prepares us to react in the best way according to the circumstances. Dread is something altogether different. It is a reaction to something beyond our control—something we might not even understand.

The only solution to dread is hope. But not baseless hope. It has to be hope rooted in something solid, dependable. So, despite my wariness as I had approached motorcycle man, I still felt no sense of impending dread. I realized I was not afraid to die. This was an epiphany for me. Something huge had changed since the day when I almost crashed with thirteen other Marines in a plunging CH-46. As the chopper veered out of control and the pilots fought to keep it airborne, I sat terrified at the prospect of my impending death.

What had changed since then? I had gained a new hope, that's what. About a year before the incident at the embassy, I had put my faith in Jesus Christ to forgive my sins and to be my Lord and Savior. I was quite literally not the same person I had been before. As God promises in the Bible, "Therefore, if anyone is in Christ, he is a new creation; the old has gone, the new has come!" (2 Corinthians 5:17).

I had the assurance that no matter what happened to me, my eternal destiny had already been decided. As we read in Psalm 91:1–5,

> *He who dwells in the shelter of the Most High*
> *will rest in the shadow of the Almighty.*

I will say of the LORD, "He is my refuge and my
  fortress,
my God, in whom I trust."
Surely he will save you from the fowler's snare
  and from the deadly pestilence.
He will cover you with his feathers,
  and under his wings you will find refuge;
  his faithfulness will be your shield and rampart.
You will not fear the terror of night, nor the arrow
  that flies by day.

I no longer had to dread death. The apostle Peter tells us, "Do not fear what they [the nonbelievers] fear" (1 Peter 3:14). He is partially quoting Isaiah 8:13, when God told the people, "The LORD Almighty is...the one you are to dread" (Isaiah 8:13). Put another way, "If God is for us, who can be against us?" (Romans 8:31).

MORE THAN MERE WORDS

You might wonder how anyone can really be sure of this. It's one thing to read it in the Bible, but deep inside, in my heart of hearts, how do I *know* it's true?

I know it's true because of God and who he is, not because of me or what I believe. The motto of the Marine Corps is *Semper Fidelis:* Always Faithful. That could be God's motto too. The story

of Scripture is a story of God's steadfast faithfulness. "Know therefore that the LORD your God is God; he is the faithful God, keeping
his covenant of love to a thousand generations of those who love
him and keep his commands" (Deuteronomy 7:9). Moses, one of
the greatest leaders and warriors in history, the former sheepherder
who emancipated a nation of slaves, knew in his heart the faithfulness of God. When things got tough in the wilderness, Moses
assured the people that "the LORD himself goes before you and will
be with you; he will never leave you nor forsake you. Do not be
afraid; do not be discouraged" (Deuteronomy 31:8). God's
promises can be trusted because he is constant. He tells us, "I the
LORD do not change" (Malachi 3:6; see also Hebrews 13:8).

Of course, this could still be just a bunch of talk. But history and
human experience—even personal experience, if you look back at
your life—confirm God's faithfulness. It just takes the right eyes to
see it. Consider, for example, the promise of Psalm 34:7: "The angel
of the LORD encamps around those who fear him, and he delivers
them." This psalm refers to the story of the prophet Elisha and his
servant, which is related in 2 Kings 6. Elisha was in the city of
Dothan, which was being besieged by Aramean forces. When
Elisha's servant awoke, he saw that the city was surrounded by enemy
soldiers and chariots. He asked his master: "What shall we do?"

"'Don't be afraid,' the prophet answered. 'Those who are with
us are more than those who are with them.' And Elisha prayed, 'O
LORD, open his eyes so he may see.' Then the LORD opened the

servant's eyes, and he looked and saw the hills full of horses and chariots of fire all around Elisha" (2 Kings 6:16–17). God sent his army of angels to deliver Elisha and the city of Dothan.

For the most part, God doesn't send an army of angels—at least not a visible army. God's care often arrives quietly, even in the form of a common bird. Take the case of Eddie Rickenbacker, the famous World War I ace who, despite his age, volunteered for service as a bomber pilot in World War II. Rickenbacker had to ditch his B-17 in the Pacific Ocean when it ran out of fuel, and he and his crew drifted for days in a life raft. They eventually were rescued, and later Rickenbacker recounted how God had provided for them: "A gull came out of nowhere," he wrote, "and lighted on my head—I reached up my hand very gently—I killed him and then we divided him equally among us. [Six men shared the life raft with Rickenbacker.] We ate every bit, even the little bones. Nothing ever tasted so good."[1] This gull saved the B-17 crew from starvation. Years after the war, Rickenbacker spoke of the incident to Billy Graham: "I have no explanation except that God sent one of his angels to rescue us," he said.[2]

In many cases, God's protection is the focus of our prayers— the prayers both of those serving in the military and of friends and family back home. Army Captain Luke Haverstick, who served a tour of duty in Iraq, described an incident in which a mortar round landed about fifteen meters from his platoon, who were standing in the open. Even though the buildings around them were peppered with shrapnel holes, "not one of my soldiers had even a slight scratch on him," Haverstick says. "I believe God had some direct intervention through the prayers of many Christians praying for me and my soldiers."

THERE ARE NO GUARANTEES AGAINST SUFFERING

Understand that while God promises to ultimately save those who call on his name, he also sometimes allows defeat, tragedy, and death. Friends and comrades die in battle or suffer disabling injuries. Why? That's a question theologians and philosophers have been wrestling with for millenniums. And since it is a question that is impossible to answer to anyone's satisfaction, we need to trust God and his faithfulness. Because he is faithful, we know that he is with us no matter how dark our circumstances.

If anyone ever had cause to doubt God, it would be the Old Testament hero Job. Here was a man whom God had blessed richly, but then disaster after disaster befell him until he lost everything— except his faith in God's faithfulness. In the midst of almost unimaginable suffering, Job spoke what I think are the ultimate words of trust: "Though he slay me, yet will I hope in him" (Job 13:15).

I actually know a man with Job-like trust in God. Marine Sergeant Les Shaw had been a Christian for only a few years when, in November 1983, he asked God to use him to help spread the gospel. Shaw didn't know when or how God might do this; he simply trusted God to use him.

Less than three months later, Shaw found himself aboard a Marine CH-53 helicopter that was ferrying troops from shore to ship as U.S. forces pulled out of Beirut, Lebanon. Returning to the beach from the ship, with only Shaw and the crew aboard, the pilot flared the helicopter too abruptly as he came in for a fast landing. The tail assembly struck the ground, causing the tail rotor to disintegrate. The huge transport helicopter slammed into the ground as razor-sharp shards of fiberglass rotor blade tore into the open back of the chopper.

"Is everyone okay?" the pilot asked over the helmet communication, or comm, system.

"Shaw's been hurt!" the door gunner shouted.

"I noticed my hand flopped over my leg," Shaw says now. The hand was held in place only by a thin piece of skin. "I picked my hand up. I thought, *I might want to keep this so they can try to put it back on.*"

A huge chunk of his leg was also missing. The crew chief hurriedly put a tourniquet on the injured leg. Shaw's flak jacket was mostly gone. A fragment of rotor blade had hit him square in the chest, causing the vest to disintegrate and leaving a huge black-and-blue mark on his breastbone. This was the same flak jacket that his staff sergeant had told him to put on "because you never know what can happen." Shaw had said he didn't think it was necessary since he was going to be aboard a helicopter, out of harm's way, but he put it on nevertheless.

Once the pain of his injury registered, Shaw said, "It felt like an eighteen-wheel rig sitting on my leg."

He was put on a stretcher and transported to an offshore Navy ship. "I realized I was back in the air," Shaw said. "I thought, *Oh, Lord, do not let this one crash!*" Even then, he thought about his earlier request that God would use him. "How was I going to honor the Lord in this new direction?"

The surgeons aboard ship and later at an Army hospital in Germany were able to save Shaw's hand. He was sent back to a Marine base in Southern California to recover. "I thought, *So this is how the Lord is going to use me, like Joni Eareckson Tada.*"[3]

Shaw's greatest concern was not his physical injuries, but that he would face his new circumstances in a way that would bring glory to God. Take, for example, the helicopter pilot. He could not apologize enough, but he was also amazed at Shaw's calm.

"I told him I didn't have any doubt that God knew this was going to happen," Shaw says. "He didn't have anything to apologize for." It gave Shaw a perfect opportunity to explain a much-quoted Bible verse: "And we know that in all things God works for the good of those who love him, who have been called according to his purpose" (Romans 8:28). The important part of that passage is the last part: "those…who have been called." Shaw explained to the pilot that you must first put your trust in God to have peace in the midst of tragedy.

Shaw was medically discharged from the Marine Corps, but not before he earned a college degree while on disability. Life continues to present challenges, including the loss of a job. Still, Shaw holds on to one particular passage of Scripture: "Dear friends, do not be surprised at the painful trial you are suffering, as though something strange were happening to you. But rejoice that you participate in the sufferings of Christ, so that you may be overjoyed when his glory is revealed.... So then, those who suffer according to God's will should commit themselves to their faithful Creator and continue to do good" (1 Peter 4:12–13, 19).

Now that's faith.

DROPPING FROM THE SKY

Air Force Captain Pete Wilkie had a perfect opportunity to put his faith into practice. One day while practicing air-combat maneuvers in his F-16 fighter, Wilkie managed to put the jet into flat spin—something that supposedly is impossible for the F-16, with its on-board computer that is designed to prevent the plane from doing anything it's not aerodynamically capable of doing. Often, a flat spin is fatal. (Think of the scene in *Top Gun* when Tom Cruise loses control of his F-14 and has to bail out; his jet was in a flat spin.)

Wilkie ran through every emergency procedure he knew as his aircraft spiraled toward the ground. "You ask yourself, 'How did I get myself into this?' I thought about ejecting, but I told myself to try one more time while I threw up one of those half-second prayers." He had fallen 12,000 feet at that point and was within a split second of having to make a fateful decision when, suddenly, he regained control of the plane.

Looking back, Wilkie summarized his experience: "You learn to trust what you know"—in this case, the emergency flight training all Air Force pilots receive. But, he added, you can't forget to pray.[4]

In times of danger, there is no better thing to do than to trust what you know. A shepherd boy named David remembered God's faithfulness in the past, when he had fought off a lion that was about to attack the sheep he was tending. Recalling God's presence during his encounter with the lion helped him face the Philistine giant, the enemy combatant named Goliath. David stated in no uncertain terms, "The LORD who delivered me from the paw of the lion and the paw of the bear will deliver me from the hand of this Philistine" (1 Samuel 17:37).

The apostle Paul, in prison and growing more certain that he would die at the hands of his Roman captors, did not fear execution because he trusted in God's saving grace. He wrote to a young disciple, Timothy, assuring him that "I know whom I have believed, and am convinced that he is able to guard what I have entrusted to him for that day" (2 Timothy 1:12).

Dietrich Bonhoeffer was one of a small group of people, mostly Christians, who stood against Hitler during World War II. Friends in

America begged him to stay with them and not return to Germany when the Nazis came to power, but Bonhoeffer knew where his duty was. He would eventually be murdered by Hitler's thugs mere days before the war ended, but there's no doubt where his hope lay:

> Do with me according to your will,
> and as is best for me.
> Whether I live or die, I am with you,
> And you, my God, are with me.
> Lord, I wait for your salvation
> And for your kingdom.[5]

I don't put myself in the same league as either Bonhoeffer or the apostle Paul, but their words help explain my epiphany that day outside the embassy in Geneva. As I approached the mysterious motorcycle man, I experienced peace in the face of danger. In Paul's words, "The peace of God, which transcends all understanding, will guard your hearts and your minds in Christ Jesus" (Philippians 4:7).

Keep God's faithfulness—his *Semper Fidelis*—in mind. It undergirds everything else in life. As we are assured in his word: "[He] will keep in perfect peace him whose mind is steadfast, because he trusts in you. Trust in the LORD forever, for the LORD, the LORD, is the Rock eternal" (Isaiah 26:3–4).

★★★★

Life Practices That Combat Fear

When you are in danger, fear is a normal reaction. God built the capacity for fear into us, to heighten our senses and prepare us to take immediate action. The surge of adrenaline is familiar to every member of the military. But the wrong kind of fear can prevent you from carrying out your mission. Here are a number of practical steps you can take to avoid feeding your fear.

1. Focus on the task. The best way to come out of a dangerous situation in one piece is to *focus*. Satan will try to distract you, but don't give him the upper hand. Command him to leave in the name of Jesus Christ (see Matthew 4:10–11).

2. Rely on your training. You have been trained by the best, so rely on your training. In high-pressure situations, you make decisions seemingly faster than the speed of rational thought. That's instinct. And good instincts are honed and sharpened by training, practice, and experience. So make the most of the training and preparation you have received—and *trust* your instincts!

3. Depend on your comrades. Several years ago the Army adopted a new recruiting slogan: "An Army of one." While it's true that it's up to *you* to perform at your very best, it's equally true that you are not alone. Your buddies are at your side. An army of one is made up of individuals fighting side by side, fighting for one another. When it comes to fighting off fear, gain strength and confidence from knowing that your comrades are there with you.

4. Draw strength from God. Memorize Bible verses that describe God's strength in times of need. Joshua 1:9 is one such verse; also see Deuteronomy 31:8 and Hebrews 13:5–6. Memorize these verses (or verses like them) and meditate on God's faithful promises as you serve in dangerous situations.

5. Find inspiring models. Study the biblical stories of legendary warriors who relied on God for wisdom and victory. Examples include Moses (Exodus 17:8–16); Joshua (Joshua 6:1–25); David (1 Samuel 17:32–51); and Gideon (Judges 7).

6. Enlist a confidant. In the macho world of the military, you might be reluctant to admit your fears. Courage is *not* the absence of fear; it's the ability to do your duty in the face of your fears. Still, it helps to have someone to talk to, someone who is honest about his own struggles. Knowing that a fellow soldier, sailor, airman, Marine, or

Coast Guardsman faces the same struggles as you goes a long way toward restoring your confidence.

7. Ask God for protection. God makes it clear that, ultimately, we are not protected by being smarter, faster, or stronger than our enemy. Yes, those are important, but in the end it's by God's power that we are safe (see Psalm 20:7). Trust in God for your protection and the protection of those you lead.

8. Reject the lies of Satan. Satan wants you to lose. In fact, he wants to destroy you (see 1 Peter 5:8–9). As a member of the armed forces, you face dual enemies: a physical enemy bent on your destruction, and Satan, the enemy of your soul. Use the truth of Scripture to reject the attacks of Satan. "The LORD is my strength and my shield; my heart trusts in him, and I am helped" (Psalm 28:7; also see Psalms 3:3; 18:30).

9. Recruit a prayer warrior. It should come as no surprise that you need the support of prayer. Find a Christian who is committed to prayer, who believes in the power of prayer, and who will serve you in prayer daily. This could be your spouse, a sibling, one of your parents, a pastor or elder, or a good friend. Ask that person to commit to holding you up in prayer every day.

3

★★★★

The Mental Burdens of Military Life

Causes of Depression and How to Find Help

Why are you downcast, O my soul?

Why so disturbed within me?

PSALM 42:5

Right after I got out of the Marines I took a job delivering furniture before starting my first year of college. The furniture store spent a bare minimum on maintenance for its used moving truck. Rather than take it to a reputable mechanic when the automatic transmission showed signs of slipping, they relied on the equivalent of a neighborhood shade-tree mechanic. One day I had the privilege of taking the truck out for deliveries right after it came back from Fly-by-Night Truck Repair.

In the middle of interstate traffic, the truck suddenly dropped out of gear. The engine screamed as it encountered no resistance from the drive train. I backed off on the gas pedal and, wedged in the middle lane of bumper-to-bumper traffic, felt the truck slowing down. I tried shifting into neutral, then back in gear. Nothing. The engine revved loudly as I tried to keep up with traffic, but finally, helplessly, I came to a halt. In the side mirrors I could see a long line of traffic backed up behind me. Cars swerved into traffic, trying to get past the sudden obstacle in the middle of the road. If dirty looks were daggers, I'd have been flayed a thousand times over.

It turned out that the man who worked on the transmission neglected to put a cap on the refill spout. The truck had been pumping out transmission fluid until there was nothing left. I spent a humiliating few hours being the cause of traffic updates on the local radio station until a tow truck could make it to me.

Sitting in a disabled truck, blocking traffic and enraging countless freeway drivers produces a helpless feeling. There are times in life that bring on the same feeling. Everything seems to drop out of gear. No matter what we try, life just seems to come to a dead halt. And many times, we don't know why.

When the bottom drops out, it's easy to lose hope. And when you lose hope, you open yourself to despondency, despair, and depression. Psychologist Archibald Hart wrote that "The incidence of depression is grossly underestimated in males, and the 'feminization' of depression has, unfortunately, not only stigmatized women in the eyes of many in the helping profession, but it has also served to prevent men from getting the help they so desperately need."[1]

Here are a few sobering statistics:

★ Men are less likely to admit to depression, and doctors are less likely to suspect it.

★ Men are four times more likely to be successful at suicide than women, even though women attempt it more often.[2]

★ Although 80 percent of people with depression who have sought help will find relief through therapy or medication (or a combination of both), fewer than one in three people who are depressed actually seeks help.[3]

The causes of depression are many, and going into the medical reasons behind it is beyond the scope of this book. But two common causes are *stress* and, ironically, *not-stress*.

First, let's look at stress. The fight-or-flight response to stress causes the adrenal glands to pump out hormones that are necessary for survival in extreme situations. But when we are under prolonged stress, these powerful hormones play havoc with our brain chemistry, that delicate balance of neurotransmitters that regulate our mood. The problem is compounded by certain personality types, particularly Type As. (And let's face it: a lot of us military-types are Type A.) Rather than dial back when we start to feel depressed, we crank up the stress. The particulars differ from one person to the next, but Hart points out that the various manifestations all represent an attempt to mask the pain. Type A responses to stress might include extreme sports, listening to loud music, or keeping busy—even busier than we were before. Adding more stress to life produces more adrenaline, compounding the chemical imbalance, increasing the depression, leading to more avoidance behaviors—on and on until we finally crash.

A second major cause of depression, *not-stress,* results when the source of stress disappears so suddenly that you have no time to decompress. Hart calls this "post-adrenaline depression."[4] The hormones are cruising at full speed through your body when, suddenly, they are not needed. But the body has built up a tolerance to the chemicals that are no longer being produced, at least not at the accustomed levels. It's like a junkie losing his supply, only this time the "drugs" are adrenaline and cortisol. When needed, they kill pain. They give us a necessary boost of energy in an emergency. When they're no longer there, we have nothing to dull the pain or give us energy. We go into a funk and, often, look for our next adrenaline fix, starting the cycle all over again.

Because most people reading this book are in the military, I'll mention a third major cause of depression that is particularly prevalent in the armed services: schedules that mess with your body clock. Guard duty, late-night patrols, and the ever-changing demands of military life mean that the ideal twenty-four-hour sequence of eight-hours-on, eight-hours-off, eight-hours-of-sleep routine is virtually unknown. This compounds the above-mentioned causes of depression, but it also means that getting proper rest can help alleviate them.

DENYING DEPRESSION

The problem with depression in the military, particularly among men, is that it is often denied. Not by the higher-ups, and definitely not by the medical corps or by chaplains; it's denied by the people who suffer from it. There's a macho mentality that you can't admit weakness. If you're a Marine, just recall the way sick call was announced each morning in boot camp: "Give me all the sick, lame, and lazy, blind, crippled, and crazy." Unless you were missing a limb or bleeding from a gaping chest wound, you didn't need a corpsman. Anyone wanting to see a doctor for less than a partial decapitation was considered a malingerer. With such an attitude inculcated from the very earliest days of military life, imagine how hard it is to seek medical help for a problem that doesn't even "bleed."

It's a stupid custom based on macho pride. But how often do we subtly believe something very similar to this? When it comes to an inner wound, we're prone to deny it. In his book *The Problem of Pain*, C. S. Lewis wrote, "Mental pain is less dramatic than physical pain, but it is more common and also more hard to bear. The frequent attempt to conceal mental pain increases the burden: it is easier to say 'My tooth is aching' than to say 'My heart is broken.'"[5]

Take the story of Lewis B. Puller Jr., the son of Lewis B. "Chesty" Puller, the most decorated Marine in the Corps' history, a hero of World War II and Korea. (During the latter war, when informed that the First Marine Division was surrounded by tens of thousands of Chinese troops at the Chosin Reservoir, Puller merely commented that that meant they could attack in any direction.) He's the closest thing to a patron saint the Marine Corps has. The Marines' mascot, a bulldog that lives at the Marine Barracks in Washington, D.C., is named Chesty. Every night in boot camp, just before hitting the rack, we recruits would say goodnight to Chesty Puller as if he were in the barracks.

Lewis Puller Jr., grew up in the very long shadow of his hero father. He joined the Marine Corps upon graduating from the College of William and Mary and soon found himself commanding an infantry platoon in South Vietnam. One fateful day in 1968, he stepped on a buried artillery round. The resulting explosion took his left leg below the knee, his right leg at the hip, his entire left hand, and portions of the right hand.

In his autobiography, *Fortunate Son,* the younger Puller wrote, "I felt guilty for years that I had abandoned [my platoon] before our work was finished. I was to feel even worse that I was glad to be leaving them and that, in my mind, I had spent my last healthy moments in Vietnam running from the enemy. [He was avoiding a squad of North Vietnamese Army regulars because his weapon had jammed.] I came to feel that I had failed to prove myself worthy of my father's name, and broken in spirit as well as body, I was going to have to run a different gauntlet."[6]

Years of depression and alcohol abuse followed. By early 1991, with the publication of his book, the younger Puller seemed to have turned a corner. I had the pleasure of meeting him at a book signing, where he sat in a wheelchair and made small talk with Marines and former Marines clamoring to be near the son of a saint. I look back at that brief encounter now and sadly realize what was going on inside him when he scrawled these words in my copy of his autobiography: "To Tom Neven, U.S.M.C. Semper Fi. Lewis B. Puller." At the time, though, I had no inkling of the anguish, both physical and mental, that he still suffered. He certainly put on a brave face during publicity events. But only months later, even after the success of his autobiography, Lewis Puller Jr. took his own life. He had never really won the battle with depression and, to the dismay of all, could not ask for help.

Denial Can Kill You

Denial is deadly. Consider, for example, what happened to a fine Christian man in another macho profession, major league baseball. Eric Show (rhymes with *pow*) won more games for the San Diego Padres than any other pitcher in the team's history. According to one-time teammate Dave Dravecky, Show was not only a great hurler, but he was a genius who knew the Bible inside out and could also discuss the works of philosophers such as Hegel and Kierkegaard. He was a natural leader and loved to share his faith. Show was, in Dravecky's words, "one studly Christian." Yet he was also hurting intensely and, rather than share his pain and seek help, Show turned to drugs.

"Eric couldn't let his guard down, lest everyone think he wasn't the person that everyone thought him to be," Dravecky writes. It was a shock to all when Show was found dead in 1994 after taking a "speedball," a toxic combination of heroin and cocaine. He was only thirty-seven years old. He died hiding his pain from the friends who would have done anything to help him.[7]

Mental pain is real. We can know, however, that our Savior, Jesus Christ, endured mental anguish unlike anything we ever will. As it says in Hebrews 4:15, "For we do not have a high priest who is unable to sympathize with our weaknesses, but we have one who has been tempted in every way, just as we are—yet was without sin." In the Garden of Gethsemane, on the night before his crucifixion, Jesus prayed earnestly, knowing what faced him the next day (see Matthew 26:36–38). Also, we read the following in Luke 22:44, "And being in anguish, he prayed more earnestly, and his sweat was like drops of blood falling to the ground"—a documented medical condition called hematohidrosis (or sometimes just hematidrosis). He feared not just death on a cross—many men had died that way—but what would be the ultimate pain for him: separation for the first time in eternity from God the Father. As Jesus bore the sins of mankind, he would feel God turn away from him (see 2 Corinthians 5:21; Matthew 27:46; Psalm 22:1–2).

Mental anguish is no stranger to God's people. The psalmist

lamented, "Why are you downcast, O my soul? Why so disturbed within me?" (Psalm 42:5). There are numerous occasions throughout Scripture where believers felt the anguish of mental pain. Elijah the prophet, one of the greatest men of faith mentioned in Scripture, suffered a period of depression (see 1 Kings 19:1–10).

Other great figures in history have struggled as well. Winston Churchill referred to his periodic bouts of depression as a "black dog" that came to visit. As is true with all metaphors, it speaks volumes. The nickname implies both familiarity with the unbidden visitor and Churchill's need to master it.

The great nineteenth century preacher Charles Spurgeon struggled with depression. And as if that weren't enough, he then had to deal with others unfairly judging his spiritual condition due to his struggle with depression. Spurgeon made the valid point that suffering from depression says nothing about you as a person. It is not a sign of weakness. It is not a sign that God is punishing you. Spurgeon wrote:

> I know that wise brethren say, "You should not give way to feelings of depression."...If those who blame quite so furiously could once know what depression is, they would think it cruel to scatter blame where comfort is needed. There are experiences of the children of God which are full of spiritual darkness; and I am almost persuaded that those of God's servants who have been most highly favoured

have, nevertheless, suffered more times of darkness than others.… No sin is necessarily connected with sorrow of heart, for Jesus Christ our Lord once said, 'My soul is exceeding sorrowful, even unto death' [Matthew 26:38, KJV]. There was no sin in Him, and consequently none in His deep depression.[8]

Indeed, sometimes it seems the most godless of men live happy-go-lucky lives while earnest followers of God struggle with mental anguish. The Old Testament prophet Jeremiah, who knew frequent times of dark despair, wrote: "You are always righteous, O LORD, when I bring a case before you. Yet I would speak with you about your justice: Why does the way of the wicked prosper? Why do all the faithless live at ease?" (Jeremiah 12:1).

DEPRESSION CAN BE HARD TO IDENTIFY

I know something of depression, myself, having experienced one bout before I became a Christian and one after. The most severe of the two occurred years *after* I had accepted Jesus as my Savior; it was preceded by a time of great blessing and was then followed by great blessing. That in-between time, though, was deep and dark, and I was sure that God had abandoned me.

Shortly after graduating from college, as I started a graduate program at Columbia University, I fell into a deep depression that lasted the better part of a year. It was, in a way, brought on by both stress and not-stress. I had just moved to New York City from a small Chicago suburb, a major life change that wasn't helped by the fact that I was moving to one of the most stressful cities in the country. The not-stress part came from the fact that I was suddenly free after four years of intense study.

The period of depression started out as general apathy. At times I had trouble sleeping; other times I couldn't get out of bed in the morning. I lost my appetite, and within a few months I had lost nearly thirty pounds. The depression fed on itself. Apathy gave way to despair, despair to feelings of doom.

At the height of the crack cocaine epidemic in the latter half of the 1980s, New York City was overrun with homeless drug addicts, people willing to do anything for their next fix. They lived on sidewalks and in subway tunnels. Here I was, a military veteran with a college degree attending one of the most prestigious graduate schools in the country, and yet so deep was my despair—and the irrationality that came with it—that I was convinced I would wind up on the streets along with the homeless. I could not imagine any other future.

Physically, I felt as if I were carrying a great weight on my back. The mental anguish finally reached its last stage: fear. After attending a midnight Christmas service, I went home and prayed earnestly for God to take away whatever it was that burdened me. But what was it?

I didn't know, because I didn't understand what was happening. I just knew something was terribly wrong. That's the case with many people. It never occurs to them that their problem is depression. Even if they suspect it, there's the stigma associated with such an illness, even though many cases of depression have a physical cause just as pneumonia or cancer has a physical cause.

Depression Caused by Not-Stress

My experience in New York was very different from my first encounter with depression, which came toward the end of First Phase of Marine boot camp. I had started to get into a groove. I was starting to feel physically fit, although I had a long way to go to get into tiptop shape. The class work on subjects as varied as first aid and military customs and courtesies actually came pretty easily for me. I even managed to be slightly less bored with close-order drill. Still, the pace was relentless and the DIs impossible to please.

And then came the ultimate disappointment: the periodic tendonitis I had suffered returned with a vengeance. During our nightly health and hygiene inspection, the company commander noted that my heel and anklebone were a big, puffy mass because of the swelling from my inflamed Achilles tendon. I was ordered to see the corpsman at sick bay the next morning. (The Navy provides chaplains and medical personnel to the Marine Corps.) The "being ordered" part is the only thing that took some of the

stigma out of it. The next morning I reported to sick bay. A corpsman hmm'ed and mumbled as he examined my swollen leg. The
previous remedy of a few days on light duty wasn't going to be
enough this time. He sent me to the main base clinic, where a
medical doctor ordered me onto indefinite light duty until the
tendon fully healed. That meant I was pulled from my training
platoon and sent to what was called the Medical Rehabilitation
Platoon, or MRP.

This at first seemed like a blessing. MRP at the time was basically time off from boot camp. By design, we recruits in MRP
weren't put under any stress. Sure, there was a DI to supervise us. But
he never yelled at us and mostly just left us alone. Our day consisted basically of meals, reading our red-covered *Marine Corps Manual* (called, for some reason, our "Little Red Monster"), polishing
our brass and boots, and shooting the breeze. Okay, it consisted
mostly of shooting the breeze.

Wow, I thought. *A vacation from boot camp!* I wrote letters to
my family informing them of my new status. (I embellished the
extent of my injury to justify being dropped from training.) I took
a leisurely shower—a true luxury on Parris Island—and then settled in to relax, at least as much as one can relax with a cast from
ankle to knee. But something funny happened. I couldn't relax. I
felt a vague sense of unease. I'd gotten exactly what I thought I'd
wanted, yet it didn't satisfy. Indeed, it made me feel worse. I fell
into a deep funk that was far worse than any physical pain.

Years later I finally understood what was so disturbing. The first, obviously, was that I had encountered not-stress. I was freed of the constant stress that is Marine boot camp. But aside from that, I realize that I was in a sort of limbo; I was accomplishing nothing. The DIs had drilled into our heads that we recruits were lower than whale excrement on the bottom of the ocean. But at least recruits had a sense of direction. They were moving toward earning the title of U.S. Marine. In MRP I had no direction, so what did that make me?

I put up a brave front in my letters home. Some of my fellow MRP recruits had already given up, and some with relatively minor injuries such as mine were already conspiring to get a medical discharge. While I mocked them for being quitters, a small voice in the back of my head urged me to join them.

I felt I had no sense of purpose. But actually I did have a purpose in MRP; it was to heal. And that's the second important lesson: sometimes God's purposes are not our purposes. His ways and his plans are not always evident to us (see Isaiah 55:8–9). In my case, rest and healing were the only way I could go forward. I had to be pulled out of the rush of daily life, or else I would constantly reinjure my tendon, which might result in a more permanent injury. (Years later I would meet a Marine C-130 pilot who had ruptured his Achilles tendon while playing racquetball, and the injury ended his flying career.)

In other words, sometimes the cure is the opposite of what we want or expect. To quote C. S. Lewis again, "Pain insists on being attended to. God whispers to us in our pleasures…but shouts in our pains: it is his megaphone to rouse a deaf world."[9]

Consider how Coast Guard rescue swimmers are trained to approach a panicky swimmer. Petty Officer Chuck Barend says, first, "You give them a verbal command to let them know who you are." Often a drowning swimmer tries to grab onto the rescuer—the wrong thing to do, since it endangers both swimmer and rescuer. "You have to take control of the situation," Barend says. "If they swim toward you, you dive under, come up behind them, and put them in a full-nelson. You try to get them to relax. If they continue to fight you, you dunk them—that gets their attention!"[10]

At times God figuratively has to put us in a wrestling hold and dunk us under some cold water to get our attention. All these years later, I'm convinced that that's what he had done to me during that year in New York. I'd grown complacent in my faith. And, what's more, I'd grown arrogant and self-satisfied during my college years, convinced I was doing so well because of something inherent in myself rather than because of God's blessing.

How do *you* respond to depression? You can continue to fight the person trying to save you, and you'll continue to get "dunked." Or you can try to figure out the problem and allow your "rescuer" to do what he's come to do. Sometimes God will point out some weakness or persistent sin in your life. You can choose to ignore the help, or you can accept it. As C. S. Lewis continued with his discussion of pain, "Yet if the cause [of the pain] is accepted and faced, the conflict will strengthen and purify the character and in time the pain will usually pass."[11]

This, by the way, does not mean you should not seek other help, such as from a chaplain or a doctor. Seeking professional help is neither a sign of weakness nor a sign that you do not trust God. Our Lord can and often does use a compassionate chaplain or a skilled doctor to accomplish his purposes.

There's another important lesson from my MRP experience. Stress is good. Not the overwhelming, relentless stress that leads to depression. But similar to the principle that muscles can grow only when they are taxed, we must constantly be pushed if we are to grow. The Russian novelist Fyodor Dostoyevsky, in his book *The House of the Dead or Prison Life in Siberia*, wrote, "If it were desired to reduce man to nothing…it would be necessary to give his work a character of complete uselessness, even to absurdity."[12] Of course, Dostoyevsky, a nineteenth-century man, could not have known of MRP, but his words nailed the experience. In my mind, my "work"—or lack of it—made me utterly useless.

The Marine Corps came to understand this too. Not long after I graduated from boot camp, MRP was revamped. Rather than relying on the mistaken notion that a stress-free environment was best for healing, they did the opposite: They *added* stress. Just a different kind. The MRP building today is filled with exercise equipment and, under the supervision of physical therapists, recruits are pushed, pulled, and stretched as their bodies heal. They are pushed academically too. The recovery rate is much higher than during my time, not only because medical science has come to understand the value of such therapy on our physical health, but also because the recruits' "work" during recovery no longer seems to be of "a character of uselessness."

If you've been unable to fight off despondency, and you suspect you are suffering from depression, whether from stress or not-stress or any other cause, *seek the help you need.* Don't continue to suffer needlessly.

★★★★

Life Practices That Combat Depression

Don't allow depression to steal your energy and rob you of concentration and focus. Take effective action to deal with it.

1. Don't let negative thoughts defeat you. It's easy to fall into a downward spiral in your thinking, especially when you are under extreme stress or when things seem to never work in your favor. But even in the midst of difficult circumstances, refuse to indulge a negative thought pattern. Interrupt negative thoughts by memorizing and meditating on verses of Scripture. The prophet Isaiah knew God's power to calm a troubled mind: "You will keep in perfect peace him whose mind is steadfast, because he trusts in you" (Isaiah 26:3). A few verses to consider are Psalm 42:5; Deuteronomy 31:8; Psalm 95:7; 119:76; 119:116; and Exodus 15:2.

2. Seek friends to help overcome feelings of isolation. You are far from home and family and serving in the most difficult circumstances of any calling in life. It's no surprise that at times you will feel isolated and

alone. And prolonged loneliness can lead to a sense of despondency. However, you can keep loneliness from producing depression. Seek a friend to do things with. You might have to take some initiative, and you might have to try a few different people before you find a friendship that really clicks, but the support you will gain from a friend makes it well worth the effort. "A friend loves at all times, and a brother is born for adversity" (Proverbs 17:17).

3. Be honest about what you're feeling. Feelings of being "down" are common and a normal part of life. It won't help to deny your feelings, so find a confidant you can talk to. A trusted listener is invaluable. It could be a chaplain, a friend, or someone from home that you can keep in touch with by e-mail.

4. Be aware of the things that trigger depression. Fatigue, the ideas and feelings that you feed your mind on, illness, hunger, long periods of stress—all of these can trigger feelings of despondency, so be aware of what is going on in your life. Once you're aware of the things that trigger negative feelings, take steps to counteract them. If you're not getting enough sleep, for example, be more disciplined about getting sleep when you can, even if it's just a power nap. It might be tempting to play that video game when you come off a late watch; it's wiser to get some shuteye.

5. Ask God to protect your mind and your emotions. Satan will do everything he can to drag you down. Remember, he wants to make you ineffective. That's why you need God's protection, encouragement, and strength to fight off negative thoughts. So commit your mind and emotions to God in prayer. God does not promise a life of ease, but he does promise his presence and his help (see Hebrews 13:5).

6. Don't let feelings rule your life. Feelings are temporary, and often they're not grounded in reality. We've all known incredibly talented people who lacked confidence when they, of all people, had reason to be more confident than others. Remember, feelings come and go. And perception often is not the same thing as reality. So don't allow your feelings to rule your life.

7. Recruit a prayer partner. Sometimes depression is a spiritual battle. Satan wants to rob you of confidence and effectiveness, so he will do everything he can to discourage you. Don't hesitate to ask a close friend to support you in prayer to the God who "gives endurance and encouragement" (Romans 15:5).

8. If your feelings of depression are prolonged and are disrupting your life, seek professional help. If you suffer from clinical depression, much of the advice contained in this chapter will be ineffective. Depression can have a physical

cause, such as a chemical imbalance brought on by long-term stress. If your depression is severe and has gripped you for an extended period, seek professional help from a chaplain or doctor.

4

★★★★

Getting the Most from Teamwork

You Are Essential, but You're Not Alone

Carry each other's burdens, and in this
way you will fulfill the law of Christ.

GALATIANS 6:2

$$\bigstar\bigstar\bigstar\bigstar$$

One of my favorite movies when I was a kid was *The 300 Spartans* starring Richard Egan as Leonidas, king of Sparta.[1] Made in 1962, the film told the true story of a small band of Greek warriors who, in 480 BC, held off a million-man Persian army at the narrow pass of Thermopylae.

The movie was fun, but also kind of hokey. It forced a Cold War grid on top of what should have been just a rousing historical action flick. (The clean-cut Spartans represented the United States and the West; the bearded Persians represented the Soviet hordes.) But that was not the film's biggest problem, at least historically speaking. The story had the Spartans fighting *mano a mano* with swords, one Spartan against one Persian, like so many other sword-and-sandal epics of the time. The Spartans were feared soldiers, but not because of their sword-fighting skills. What made them so formidable was the *phalanx.*

The Spartan phalanx was a battlefield innovation that consisted of a solid wall of interlocked shields as many as twelve rows deep. The soldiers, called hoplites, carried long spears that extended beyond the front rank. With shields locked together to form a wall, the Spartans trotted forward and crashed into the enemy force en masse. The Spartans in the front row of the phalanx, using shorter spears, jabbed over the tops of their shields. They moved in unison—hey, early close-order drill!—with flutes or pipers keeping the beat as the entire mass of sharp points, armor, and shields surged inexorably forward.

The image of a steamroller comes to mind, and for good reason. The Greek phalanx steamrollered numerous enemies. It's the only way a relatively small band of Greeks could hold off the numerically superior Persians. Alas, the Spartans were eventually betrayed. A Greek sheepherder showed the Persians a narrow path through the mountains, which enabled them to come up behind the Spartans. Surrounded, the Spartans couldn't rely on their normal tactics and they were eventually brought down by a rain of arrows from all directions. (When warned that the Persians' arrows would darken the sky, Leonidas commented, "Good, then we can fight in the shade.")[2] They did buy enough time, though, to allow other Greek armies to rally and eventually defeat the Persian invasion at the battle of Salamis.

SIDE BY SIDE, AND EQUAL

Military historian Victor Davis Hanson, author of *The Western Way of War: Infantry Battle in Classical Greece,* notes that the phalanx, as formidable as it was, would not have been successful without two additional elements: each hoplite's disciplined refusal to break ranks with his brothers and the sense of equality all Greeks shared, from general to foot soldier, as they fought side by side. Compare that to how the Persians fought. Xerxes, king of the Persians, sat on his golden throne on a hill above the battle as he sent his men to die for him. The Persian soldiers were no doubt brave, but they did not have a leader who shared in what they were experiencing. In contrast, Leonidas and other Greek generals fought in the front rank alongside their soldiers. They sweated and bled just as their men did.

The U.S. military has a long history of such camaraderie. One example that comes to mind occurred during the Battle of the Bulge in World War II. The German attack caught the U.S. army troops off-guard. As German panzer units drove deep into American lines, entire units were cut off and scattered. Many an army would have broken, but not the Americans. Small bands of men from different outfits came together and formed impromptu units that fought the Germans as best they could. They weren't big, but their delaying actions succeeded in slowing down the Nazi offensive until the Allies could regroup and counterattack. In the meantime, the soldiers of Bastogne, knowing they sat on a vital crossroads, grimly held on as they were pounded by German artillery and panzer units, refusing to give up the crucial town. The individual soldiers, in effect, locked shields and stood fast. Colonels and privates fought alongside one another for a common good.

The stereotype of the military, seen often in Hollywood fare such as *A Few Good Men,* is of high-ranking officers lording it over enlisted men and women and of sergeants getting results by demeaning their troops. Anyone who has served knows this is far from the truth. Generally speaking, I have found that the higher the rank, the more humble and soft-spoken the leader. Promotion boards have a way of weeding out blow-hards and glory hogs.

Of course, the military is a hierarchical organization. It functions because some people have more responsibility than others, and with responsibility comes privileges. Yet here's the important point: None has greater *worth* than the other. All are equally worthy of respect. All are equally soldiers, sailors, airmen, Marines, or Coast Guardsmen.

If you think about it, the Trinity functions in the same way. God the Father, God the Son, and God the Holy Spirit are all equally God in essence and in their worthiness to be worshipped, yet even within the Trinity is a hierarchy of sorts. God the Father sends the Son (see John 5:37), and the Father and the Son send the Spirit (see John 15:26). The Son prays to the Father and is obedient to his will (see Luke 22:42). The Father gives us to his Son (see John 10:29), and the Father alone knows the time of Jesus' return (see Matthew 24:36).

God Among Us

Like Leonidas, the ancient king of Sparta, our Lord knows what it is like to sweat and bleed alongside us. Jesus was God himself, yet during his life on earth he was willing to humble himself for our sake. I've known many a fine officer who, whether he knew it or not, lived out this same ideal:

Each of you should look not only to your own interests, but also to the interests of others. Your attitude should be the same as that of Christ Jesus:

Who, being in very nature God,
did not consider equality with God something
to be grasped,
but made himself nothing,
taking the very nature of a servant,
being made in human likeness.

And being found in appearance as a man,
  he humbled himself
  and became obedient to death—
    even death on a cross! (Philippians 2:4–8).

Jesus, the greatest leader of all time, whose life did more to change the world than any other, also practiced humility like no other person who ever lived. There is a crucial lesson here for other leaders who want their lives to have maximum impact. While military rank gives you certain privileges, you should accept these humbly. Peter the apostle also was commissioned for duty, receiving his commission directly from the Lord (see John 21:17). Yet listen to how he expressed his authority:

> To the elders among you, I appeal as a fellow elder, a witness of Christ's sufferings and one who also will share in the glory to be revealed: Be shepherds of God's flock that is under your care, serving as overseers—not because you must, but because you are willing, as God wants you to be; not greedy for money, but eager to serve; not lording it over those entrusted to you, but being examples to the flock.
> (1 Peter 5:1–3)

Peter, whose name lives on as one of the greatest leaders of the early church, calls himself a "fellow elder." He encourages leaders to be servants and to serve as examples to others, rather than "lording it over" those who serve under them.

A Leader, Not a Lord

The example of Leonidas and other Spartan leaders is inspiring, but today's military is a much different organization. Generals command units of brigade size or larger, so they cannot be in the frontline with their men. I remember an illustration from the Basic School, which all Marine second lieutenants must attend upon being commissioned. The newly minted officers are given an exercise to erect a large flagpole within a certain period of time. Inevitably the natural leaders take charge of the exercise, and everyone sweats and grunts trying to get the pole in place within the required time limit.

Most groups fail to achieve the goal, but even those who manage to get the flagpole more or less perpendicular to the ground fail the exercise. Why? Because upon being given the command by their captain—"Lieutenant, I want that flagpole erect by thirteen hundred hours!"—the solution is not for the lieutenants to erect the pole. The proper answer, almost always missed, is to turn and say, "Sergeant, I want that flagpole erect by twelve-forty-five" and to *supervise* the project. The sergeant, in turn, might task a corporal to find and supervise the men who will do the actual work. The lieutenant cannot lead the platoon if he's down in the dirt digging a hole or filling the base with rock. Neither can the sergeant lead the squad if he's doing the grunt work. The old adage holds true: Leaders lead. They also take responsibility. If for some reason the pole isn't up at thirteen-hundred, the captain is not going to chew out the sergeant or the corporal; he'll chew out the lieutenant.

The responsibility of leadership does not make the lieutenant or sergeant better than other soldiers because they sometimes lead without getting their hands dirty. It just means they are fulfilling the role their rank gives them. It's one of those paradoxes of leadership. Remember, all are of equal worth—especially in the eyes of God.

In the end, the difference between worth (all are equal) and function (leaders lead) is one of attitude. Peter could not possibly be the leader of every congregation that made up the early church. That's why he and the other apostles appointed elders to lead individual bodies of believers. But even though Peter couldn't in every instance get down in the dirt with them, so to speak, he did not consider himself better than them. As the apostle Paul wrote, "Do not think of yourself more highly than you ought.... Just as each of us has one body with many members, and these members do not all have the same function, so in Christ we who are many form one body, and each member belongs to all the others" (Romans 12:3–5).

Unfortunately, not everyone thinks this way. I worked with a colonel whose disdain for enlisted men was palpable, which was ironic considering he had once been an enlisted man. I knew enlisted men who resented the fact that officers tend to get more medals than enlisted men, mainly, they perceive, because officers write the medal recommendations and tend to favor those who are most like themselves. I understand that resentment, by the way, and in all honesty have felt it myself. But here's another opportunity where the Christian ideal should show us the way to go.

A military unit is like a human body. Without sergeants, corporals, and privates, the senior officers could not function, for as Paul wrote elsewhere:

The body is a unit, though it is made up of many parts;...
If the foot should say, "Because I am not a hand, I do not
belong to the body," it would not for that reason cease to be
part of the body.... If the whole body were an eye, where
would the sense of hearing be? If the whole body were an
ear, where would the sense of smell be?... The eye cannot
say to the hand, "I don't need you!" And the head cannot
say to the feet, "I don't need you!" (1 Corinthians 12:12,
15, 17, 21).

What makes the U.S. military strong is the fact that, if necessary, *everyone* gets dirty. Like Leonidas leading the Spartans, sometimes every warrior, no matter his rank, gets into the thick of it. Consider, for example, General Anthony McAuliffe, who commanded the 101st Airborne, which was among the units surrounded at Bastogne during the Battle of the Bulge. (Despite his heroism, he is most famous for his single-word reply to a German surrender ultimatum: "Nuts!") He chose to stay with his division even as it was being cut off by German troops.[3]

THE PROBLEM OF RACISM

As much as we talk about the power of teamwork and the necessity of each member of the unit being given equal respect and regard, there remains a problem of disunity in the military. The most glaring example of a lack of brotherhood in the ranks is the blot of racism. The problem persists, even though the military in many respects led the way in becoming one of society's first bastions of racial equality.

One reason race becomes an issue is that military service throws together people who would not normally meet and interact—cowboys from Texas serving alongside urban dwellers from Jersey City and surfer dudes from California. In the 1970s, this proved to be a combustible mixture, especially as it touched on racial differences, since most members in the military came from largely segregated neighborhoods.

A day before I graduated from boot camp, one of our drill instructors called the platoon aside for an important discussion: "I want to warn you about a problem you might encounter once you graduate from here," he said gravely. The problem he spelled out was the wave of racial infighting that plagued the Corps in the years immediately following the Vietnam War, a problem still unresolved in 1975.

"Some are going to pressure you to be a black Marine or a white Marine," the DI said. "Well, there's no such thing. There are only green Marines. Don't fall into their trap. We're all on the same team. Marines."

It was a harsh awakening to a hard reality. *You mean Marines actually hate each other?* I thought. *Marines actually fight or try to kill one another?* After all the lessons of esprit, pride, camaraderie, and teamwork, the DI had thrown us a curve.

And sadly, I saw his warning lived out. When I was stationed at Camp Hansen on Okinawa, we had to be patted down by MPs at the main gate *before* going into town, a move prompted by several racially motivated fights in the town of Kin (or Kin-ville, as we called it). Indeed, this Japanese town was unofficially segregated, with some bars catering to black Marines by playing soul and R&B music and other establishments courting white Marines with either hard rock or country music.

The worst came when, as sergeant of the guard, I had to write up a Marine for being drunk and disorderly. He happened to be black, but that had no bearing on why I put charges on him. He came into the barracks late at night, drunk, and turned on his stereo full blast. (This was in the days of open squad bays, which had simple wooden dividers between cubicles, so his music woke everyone up.) After the first warning, he turned off the stereo and climbed into the rack. I wasn't ten steps outside the barracks before the music came back on. He did the same thing after the second warning, so I told him I was going to write him up in the company logbook and, if he did it one more time, I was calling the MPs.

I got back to my post and started my log entry—fortunately I'd written his name down at that point—when he came charging in with a pair of nunchakus. It was pretty stupid on his part, as I had a loaded .45 on my hip, but I had no time to draw it. He knocked me cold, splattering blood across the company office. (It looked more serious than it was, as scalp wounds bleed a lot, but it still took thirty-plus stitches to close the wound.) The Marine Corps charged him with attempted murder, as another Marine heard him verbalize a threat to kill me and because nunchakus are considered a deadly weapon. As far as I know, he's still serving a life sentence in Leavenworth.

Still, even though I was justified in writing up the drunk Marine, I was eventually transferred to another battalion because none of the other black Marines would have anything to do with me. It proved easier to move one sergeant than to move every black Marine in the company. It's scary to think what would have happened if our unit had been sent into combat. We were anything but a band of brothers.

Thankfully, the military has made great strides in dealing with race-related issues, but recently I read about the presence of gangs within the Army. Gang graffiti have appeared on latrine walls and even on military equipment in Iraq. Army officials tacitly admit to the presence of gang members serving in the military in Iraq, but they insist that those soldiers set aside their differences when it comes to fighting the common enemy, the insurgents or Islamic terrorists. But I wonder how long that can last. It has started to affect military cohesion stateside too. Officers have to carefully consider plans to move some units from Fort Hood, Texas, to Fort Bliss, Texas, because Fort Hood personnel connected with Chicago-based gangs will clash with personnel affiliated with Hispanic gangs at Fort Bliss.[4]

Racial hatred, gang beefs, or just plain discord within the ranks is a blight on the military. This is a case where the Christian ideal should rule. The Body of Christ consists of men and women from every continent, speaking myriad languages and influenced by hundreds of cultures. Yet we all profess the same Lord. The apostle Paul wrote, "There is neither Jew nor Greek, slave nor free, male nor female, for you are all one in Christ Jesus" (Galatians 3:28). The early church faced potential divisions between the Jews of Jerusalem, Judea, and Samaria and the gentiles of the larger world, referred to generically as Greeks. The Jewish Christians also were persecuted by the Romans. And yet the church spread like wildfire because the early Christians obeyed Jesus' command: "Love one another. As I have loved you, so you must love one another. By this all men will know that you are my disciples, if you love one another" (John 13:34–35). The church became a culture-changing force. The pagan Roman Empire that covered most of the known world was Christianized in the course of only a few hundred years, turning the world upside down.

Why Trust Is Essential

When discord rules, the missing component is trust. Trust is what makes the military function. The pilot sitting in his F/A-18 perched on a carrier flight deck must have absolute trust in the men and women who scramble around his plane checking all the control surfaces and hooking the front landing gear to the catapult that will hurl him off the ship. A squad of soldiers preparing to do a take-down of a room in Iraq must each have absolute trust in the man to his left, right, and behind him.

A spectacular example of trust can be seen in what is probably the ultimate in close-order drill: the Marine Corps' Silent Drill Platoon, stationed at the oldest post in the Corps, the Marine Barracks at Eighth & I in Washington, D.C. The basic maneuvers we tried to perfect in boot camp could be done sleepwalking by the Silent Drill Platoon. The twenty-four Marines of the Silent Drill Platoon perform intricate marching maneuvers while twirling their ten-and-a-half-pound M1 Garand rifles—with fixed bayonets and without a single command being uttered.

These are not fake bayonets, either. They're long, and they're sharp. One movement is called a "secure," in which the ranks of Marines face each other and each fourteen-and-one-half-inch bayonet is placed within one inch of the opposite Marine's ear. The Marines then perform a series of maneuvers and spins with their rifles. Each must know absolutely that his opposite partner has his head in the game. Likewise, he cannot flinch or move. That's trust.

It's the same trust you have to have in your fellow soldiers, sailors, airmen, Marines, or Coast Guardsmen. It's the same trust you have to have in the officers appointed over you. And, most important, it's the same trust you have to have in your ultimate Commanding Officer. He is not like the Persian king Xerxes, who ruled from on high, impervious to the pain and suffering of his army. You can think of Jesus as more like King Leonidas of the Spartans, taking his place in the front rank with his men. He knows what it's like to be tired, to bleed and sweat, to be afraid. And that makes Jesus a Leader worth following.

★★★★

Life Practices That
Strengthen Teamwork

A military unit is made up of individuals, so take some time to
look at yourself and your place in the bigger picture. What type
of team member are you? Do you get maximum benefit from
teamwork?

1. Strengthen your reliance on others. The natural human
   tendency is to go it alone, to rely on yourself and not
   seek the assistance of others. But no one, no matter
   how smart, talented, or well-trained, can succeed
   alone. Military training instills this truth, but it's easy
   to lose sight of the power you gain when you partner
   with others. To counteract this natural tendency, stop
   to think how others contribute to your success. If
   you're a "list person," write down the names of five
   men and women who serve with you, and beside each
   name indicate one way that he or she makes a critical
   contribution to your effectiveness and success.

2. Be aware of pride and its damaging effects. One reason
   we are tempted to think we don't need others is the
   basic human problem of pride. Pride, in fact, is what

got Lucifer thrown out of heaven. He wanted to be equal to God, rather than to serve God (see Isaiah 14:12–14). Ask God to show you ways in which you tend to seek greater recognition or honor than your comrades.

3. Ask for help. As an experiment, during the next week find ways to get the maximum benefit from the help of a friend. This is a legitimate way to "take advantage" of another person. Think of a friend who has offered to help you. This could be just about anything—help with moving, repairing your car, cleaning out your garage, painting a room, organizing your finances. Let your friend know that you'd like to take him or her up on the offer of help, and then enjoy the benefits. It's as simple as that.

4. Gain inspiration from God's Word. Read the passages in Romans 12:3–8 and 1 Corinthians 12:12–27, which describe the various members of the church as different parts of the same body. This metaphor is helpful when you consider the teamwork that is necessary for effective performance in the military. As you read the passages, picture yourself and the specific functions that you serve, how you assist others, and the ways in which your role is essential to the success of the whole. Thank God for giving you the tasks, roles, and responsibilities that are yours.

5. Enhance teamwork through gratitude. Since you and your teammates succeed by working together, remember to be

thankful for those on your team. If you listed the names of five people in your unit as a result of the first question above, review that list and recall how each person helps you achieve your objectives. Now, within the next week, make it a point to thank each of those people for what they contribute.

6. Check your trust quotient. Teams can't function without trust. If you don't trust the man or woman serving beside you, the power of the team is diminished. With that in mind, conduct a quick self-inventory on trust. In what areas do you have trouble trusting a teammate to do his or her job? What lies behind that lack of trust? In what ways do you fail to trust yourself? In what ways is it hard to trust God? How can you overcome the influences that cause you to doubt your teammates, yourself, and God?

7. Examine your role on the team. The best teams are greater than the sum of their parts. Your role in the group is as important as everyone else's. I once served with a major who shared this bit of wisdom: "No one is smarter than all of us." Your effort and contribution are important not only because they reflect on your character, but also because they contribute to the success of the unit. Think about your individual role and reflect on how you contribute uniquely to the success of the group.

8. Maximize prayer through teamwork. Jesus said, "If two of

you on earth agree about anything you ask for, it will be done for you by my Father in heaven" (Matthew 18:19). There is power in numbers, even when it comes to prayer. Ask a few friends to join you weekly for a time of prayer. Keep a list of your prayer requests and God's answers to your prayers. Review the list from time to time and thank God for his answers.

9. Ask God to supply the discipline you lack. God calls you to a task, and then he equips you for it. No one is a self-made man or woman. And nowhere is this more true than in the military. Not only do you depend on your comrades in arms, you depend ultimately on God. Without his power to overcome your natural bent to pride and self-centeredness, you would fail at just about everything you attempt. The self-giving attitude that is necessary for successful teamwork comes straight from God (see Philippians 2:4–8). Ask God to help you develop the self-giving attitude that leads to success.

10. Ask God to hold you accountable. Left to your own devices, it's easy to rationalize a tendency to look out for yourself first and foremost. Ask God to open your eyes to your tendency toward self-interest (see Psalm 139:23–24).

5

Taking Control of Your Finances

How to Make Your Money Work for You

The borrower is servant to the lender.

PROVERBS 22:7

S he was a beaut. A 1976 Dodge pickup. Six cylinders under the hood, three on the tree. An eight-track stereo tape player built right into the dash! And I paid all of $1,400 for her—new. That's right. In 1976, a mere $1,400 got you a brand-new pickup truck.

It was big money to me at the time. When I'd enlisted in the Marines, I volunteered for the infantry, which meant I got a $1,500 bonus. By the time I finished boot camp, infantry school, and then Sea School, I'd been in the Corps for more than six months. It was time to reward myself.

The senior sergeant of the Marine detachment aboard the USS

Puget Sound took me around the Norfolk area to shop for a pickup. (I didn't seriously consider buying a car; it had to be a pickup with a camper shell on the back.) Upon signing all the papers, I wrote a check to the car dealer. The truck was mine, cash on the barrel head.

I cherished that little Dodge, washing her religiously and spending hours applying a fine white pinstripe to her copper-colored curves. You'd think I would have kept that truck forever. After all, it was paid for. But no. I got restless for new wheels. Within six months I was shopping for another pickup.

I went into a Ford showroom, and she caught my eye immediately. A Ford 150 pickup with a stepside bed. A big 302 under the hood and extra-wide tires on five-spoke, chromed mag wheels. I think I actually drooled. *Buy me!* she whispered. A small voice in the back of my mind reminded me that I had a perfectly good pickup truck that was already paid for. *Buy me!* she whispered again. This truck cost a lot more than my Dodge—almost $5,000. The salesman told me that if I traded in the Dodge I could finance the balance.

By day's end, my Dodge pickup with her painstaking pin-striping and genuine eight-track stereo was headed for the used-car lot, and I was wheeling around town in a new Ford with a big engine, wide tires, mag wheels—and a hefty bank note. I'm surprised I got the financing, considering my lance corporal's (E-3) pay. But the car dealer knew something about suckers like me; he could always lean on Uncle Sam to get me to pay. It is, after all, a violation of the Uniform Code of Military Justice to skip out on a debt. A call to my commanding officer would be all that was necessary to rectify things should I miss a payment.

Not that that was a problem. I dug deep into my lance corporal's paycheck each month and made my truck payment. Sure, I spent a lot of time in the barracks because I couldn't afford to do anything else, but, hey, I had a roof over my head and scintillating Marine mess hall food—and a really cool Ford pickup that stayed parked a lot because I couldn't afford to go out.

Within months I was sent on a one-year tour to Okinawa, so I left my very expensive baby with my parents in Florida. Upon returning to the States, I reclaimed the truck and drove it cross-country to Twentynine Palms in California. Along the way I ran out of gas in West Texas because the thing was such a gas hog. And guess what else happened. Only a few months after getting settled at my new base, I started to get restless with my wheels again. Next thing I knew, I'd bought a new Toyota pickup. Two years' worth of payments on the Ford went for naught, as I wound up financing the Toyota for more than I owed on the Ford.

The Real Cost of Debt

Sure, I was getting nice new pickups every few years, but in the process I was digging myself deeper into debt. I went from owning a perfectly good pickup outright to having…well, a perfectly good pickup plus a load of debt. Which calls to mind a bit of wisdom from that great philosopher John Wayne. Playing his classic role as the tough Marine Sergeant Stryker in *Sands of Iwo Jima*, the Duke said, "Life is tough. It's tougher when you're stupid."[1]

When it came to cars and money, was I stupid! I take small comfort, though, in knowing that I was in good company. I know someone who bought a brand-new Toyota Celica every year. Yeah, he had that nice new-car smell to greet him each morning, but he also had permanent car payments. And it's not always about cars. When it comes to money, some otherwise very smart people suddenly become very stupid. For them, money is not a tool but a drug. The great boxer Joe Louis once said of money, "I don't necessarily like it, but it quiets my nerves."[2]

A family resources specialist who works with the Coast Guard in Alaska describes two Coasties who had contrasting perspectives on money. One member took in a roommate and saved his excess housing allowance for a down payment on a condo. Now he lives in the condo with another roommate and is saving for a house.

Another member of the same crew described his strategy: "I ate bologna sandwiches on white bread for lunch and dinner every day to save money."

"Wow, that was a pretty big sacrifice," the specialist said. "What were you saving for?"

"Beer and guns," the Coast Guardsman said as his crewmates

hooted with laughter.

The first man gave up a little privacy so he could buy a home; the second gave up good food—and possibly several years of health!—to buy beer and guns.

Money: Practical Tool or Idol?

The Bible has a lot to say about our attitude toward wealth. Actually, the Bible is often misquoted to say, "Money is the root of all evil." But the truth is that money itself is neutral—neither good nor bad. Money is merely a tool. Scripture, in fact, says, "For the *love* of money is a root of all kinds of evil. Some people, eager for money, have wandered from the faith and pierced themselves with many griefs" (1 Timothy 6:10).

Loving an object—money, possessions, any kind of "stuff"— more than God is a form of idolatry. What is first in your life? God? Money? Stuff? Money *and* stuff, but not God?

The Bible tells a story that illustrates the point well. Jesus is confronted by a wealthy young man who asks, "Good teacher, what must I do to inherit eternal life?" (Luke 18:18). Jesus tells him he must keep all the commandments.

"All these I have kept since I was a boy," the rich young ruler answers.

But has he? Jesus then says, "You still lack one thing. Sell everything you have and give to the poor, and you will have treasure in heaven. Then come, follow me." At these words the young man "became very sad, because he was a man of great wealth" (Luke 18:21–23).

The story continues, "Jesus looked at him and said, 'How hard it is for the rich to enter the kingdom of God! Indeed, it is easier for a camel to go through the eye of a needle than for a rich man to enter the kingdom of God'" (Luke 18:24–25).

Now, a few things this passage is *not* saying. It's not telling everyone they must sell everything they own. Jesus knew what this particular man needed to hear, and that's why he prefaced his advice by telling the man he must keep all the commandments. The man thought he had done that, but clearly he was violating the first commandment: "I am the LORD your God....You shall have no other gods before me" (Exodus 20:2–3).

The man, whether he realized it or not, had made a god of his wealth. Jesus, in his inimitable way, got to the heart of the matter. If the man wanted to inherit eternal life, he must worship the true God, not the financial idol he had created. (This story also illustrates the subtlety of sin, by showing how easily we slip into sin without realizing it.)

YOUR ATTITUDE TOWARD MONEY AND DEBT

Here's another thing the story does *not* say. Some have tried to soften Jesus' teaching on the potentially corrupting power of wealth. They say Jesus was referring to an obscure gate in the walls of Jerusalem called the Eye of the Needle, which was small and narrow. A camel would have a hard time making it through, but if it struggled just so, it could fit. Well, there is *zero* archaeological or historical evidence that such a gate existed. No, Jesus was using hyperbole—deliberate exaggeration for effect—as he often did to make a point, to wit: the rich tend to be satisfied with their riches and don't see their need for God. They have made an idol of their wealth, and just like the young man in the story, they miss what it is they need to do to inherit eternal life.

To be sure, there are plenty of poor people and in-between people who have this same problem. And *rich* is a relative term. One man defined it as just a thousand dollars more than he currently had. God has blessed some people with great wealth, which many of them use to further his kingdom. The real issue is your attitude toward money and possessions.

Do you have to have the latest, the best, the coolest? Do you go into unnecessary debt to get more and better stuff? I qualify that question with the word *unnecessary* because in today's world, there are some things the average person can't buy without borrowing, especially a house. Some people must also borrow money to buy a car.

But do you go into debt without needing to, to satisfy your wants and not your needs? There is one inescapable fact about debt: "The borrower is servant to the lender" (Proverbs 22:7).

Until you pay off a loan, you always have to dance to the tune the lender calls.

Imagine yourself as a prisoner of war. You are not at liberty to move about as you want. You can't determine your own schedule, you must be careful what you say, and you are held against your will and forbidden from talking to your fellow prisoners. You are not serving under the orders of your commanding officer but existing as a slave in chains, a captive of the enemy. King Solomon knew what he was talking about when he observed that the borrower is the servant of the lender. Do you want to be imprisoned by a financial institution, unable to exercise the freedom of a person who is not indebted to anyone? The choice is yours.

By taking on unnecessary debt you also are stealing from yourself. You're spending tomorrow's money today, which means that future needs—and wants—are delayed or prohibited by today's spending. Every penny you pay in interest today is a penny you won't have to spend tomorrow. And the interest you pay in order to grab that "great deal" today usually means that it turns out to be not such a good deal after all. It's one thing to invest in something that will increase in value, such as a house. It's another to take on debt to buy something that will decrease in value. That cool car you just have to have loses a huge chunk of value the moment you drive it off the lot. That Xbox 360 will never fetch as much money as you spent for it, even before you factor in interest payments.

★★★★

Life Practices That
Lead to Financial Success

Here are eight financial lessons that I and others have learned, sometimes the hard way. Take these to heart so you won't end up making the same mistakes.

1. The bank takes its chunk of cash first. Any time you finance a purchase, the interest is front-loaded so that the bank makes its profit first. Depending on the amount of the loan, the term, and the interest rate, your early payments could be almost entirely interest, with only a tiny fraction going to pay off the amount borrowed (the principal). If for some reason the item you bought has to be repossessed, the bank will have already made its money on your interest payments and will recoup a portion of the remaining principal owed by selling the house, car, furniture, or motorcycle that you financed. In the end, the bank doesn't stand to lose much, but you stand to lose a lot if you're unable to make your payments due to taking on too much debt. And that's all before you consider what a repo looks like on your credit report.

2. Pay attention to the interest rate and the term of the loan. Don't be fooled by salesmen who try to sell you a more expensive car by emphasizing the "affordable monthly payments." Sometimes they stretch out the term of the loan in order to bring the monthly rate down, but that means you pay more in interest. If you finance that nice $20,000 car so that you pay only around $275 per month, you will shell out $27,142 before the loan is paid off. (That's figuring an 8 percent interest rate for eight years.) But think about the original price of the car. Would you pay almost $30,000 for a $20,000 car? On the other hand, if you had saved up in advance and paid cash for the car, you would have paid $7,000 less. Plus, you would have owned the car right from the start.

Another benefit to saving up in advance, rather than taking out a costly auto loan, is that whenever you pay cash for something, you often will decide to buy a less-expensive item. Paying cash might convince you to buy a reliable but less-flashy $12,000 car rather than a newer and sportier $20,000 model.

3. Compare the scheduled loan payments with the depreciating value of the car. Since an automobile is a depreciating item, borrowing money to buy it can result eventually in you owing more in outstanding principal than the car is currently worth. If you check an amortization schedule

on the loan and compare it to the rate of depreciation on the car's value over the term of the loan, you will see that before you have paid off the loan the amount of principal you still owe might exceed the current value of the car. (That's called being "upside down" on a loan.) Check out Kelley Blue Book at www.kbb.com to see sample depreciation rates on different makes and models of cars.

4. Beware of balloon payments. On some loans, particularly mortgages and home equity loans, you pay a seemingly reasonable amount early in the life of the loan and then, suddenly, a large lump-sum payment is due. But what if you can't make the payment? The bank gets back the item you purchased plus all the interest you have already paid, or else you have to refinance the loan at terms that are much more favorable to the bank.

5. Avoid "rent to own" arrangements. Most states have laws governing how much interest a business can charge. (Even then, sky-high interest rates still are allowed for certain businesses, such as credit card companies.) Some businesses get around the legal limits set on interest rates by calling interest charges "rental fees." Rent-to-own furniture, electronics, and appliance companies, for example, might offer to rent you a living room suite for $150 a month for, say, five years, after which you will own the furniture. Sounds tempting if you don't have $2,500 on hand to buy

the set up-front. But if you agree to the rent-to-own arrangement, after five years you will have paid *$9,000* for furniture that was worth $2,500 new, and much less after you have used it for sixty months. That's an exorbitant interest rate, but under the terms of a rent-to-own arrangement it's considered a rental fee. The company has ripped you off—legally.

A variation on this is the offer made by certain frozen-foods companies that deliver steaks and burgers to your home so long as you rent a freezer from them. You think you're getting a good deal on the meat until you calculate how much interest you pay on the freezer through "rental fees."

6. Filing for bankruptcy is a fool's errand. Keep in mind that recent changes to the bankruptcy law make it much harder to use bankruptcy to erase your debt. Yes, there are circumstances where an individual or family must file for bankruptcy, often because of the crippling cost of medical care associated with chronic illness, debt incurred as a result of long-term unemployment, or the loss of income after the death or injury of a spouse. But the days of simply wiping away your debts because you got in over your head are gone. And if for some reason you do file bankruptcy, it can keep you from obtaining future financing for, say, a house. It can also prevent you from

getting certain jobs or sometimes even a promotion. (A friend lost his chance at a management position with a large restaurant chain when they found out he had filed for bankruptcy years earlier.)

7. Even if you're convinced you need something right now, you probably don't. This is where self-discipline comes in. There are very few things that any of us needs *right now.* More often, we're too lazy or too impatient to wait and save up the money to get it. I write this advice knowing that it touches on my personal weakness. The Coast Guard family resources specialist mentioned earlier shares valuable wisdom in this area. When offering a course on financial planning, she asked some of the Coasties how they saved money. One burly young man raised his hand. "I feel kind of stupid about this," he said, "but it has worked for me." He pulled out his wallet, which contained an advertisement for a pickup truck. He explained that whenever he was out shopping and saw something he wanted to buy, he took out the truck photo and reminded himself that he needed to save money for that future purchase. Now that's great discipline.

8. A credit card can work for you—but only if you're smart. With more and more commerce taking place over the Internet, and certain other transactions requiring payment by credit card, it's hard to function on a cash-only basis.

Try making an airline or hotel reservation without a credit card. Good luck. Or see what happens when your car breaks down miles from home and you try to pay for repairs with a personal check. You need a major credit card. But be smart and use it to your advantage. Don't fall into the trap of paying interest on your balance.

Make your credit card work *for* you by paying off the balance in full every month. (I know one woman who, every time she uses her credit card, writes down the amount of the purchase in her checkbook register, as if she had written a check for that amount. When she later pays the credit card bill with a check, she has already deducted the amount from her checking account balance. That way she avoids spending the money twice.) Also, use a credit card that has a rewards program, such as accumulating frequent flyer miles with an airline. (Get a card that will allow you to use the miles on more than one airline.)

I realize that with some big, unexpected expenses, such as your transmission falling apart in the middle of Nevada, you might not be able to pay off your credit card bill in full the first month. Whatever you do, though, do not merely pay the minimum amount required. That approach multiplies your debt by charging interest on existing interest for every month you delay paying off the balance.

This chapter provides a quick overview of some of the financial traps that many of us fall into. You can gain additional financial wisdom by reading *Taming the Money Monster,* by Ron Blue, and *The Debt Diet,* by Ellie Kay.

In the end, it comes down to this: who serves whom? Have money and stuff become gods to you? Do you have the same problem as the rich young ruler who confronted Jesus in Luke 18? Jesus understood the lure of money and materialism. That's why he warned, "No one can serve two masters. Either he will hate the one and love the other, or he will be devoted to the one and despise the other. You cannot serve both God and Money" (Matthew 6:24).

If you make smart choices, you can avoid becoming a servant to money.

6

★★★★

God's Rules for Great Sex

You'll Be Happier and Healthier if You Get Smart About Sex

But among you there must not be even a
hint of sexual immorality.

EPHESIANS 5:3

The U.S. Navy base at Subic Bay, Philippines, used to be a desired port of call or, better yet, permanent duty station. Sun! Sand! Sex!

While Subic Bay and the nearby Naval Air Station at Cubi Point were situated in one of the most beautiful places on the planet, that's not why generations of sailors and Marines wanted to go there. Time at Subic meant only one thing: visits to the town of Olongapo. Just a few steps outside the main gate, across a small bridge spanning a river nicknamed for the raw sewage that flowed into it, you were on the main drag of sex central. Main street Olongapo was about a mile long and lined with bars, strip joints, movie theaters, and food vendors. The bars and strip joints were full of girls who would take you home and offer unlimited sex for just a few pesos. Long before Las Vegas coined the obnoxious phrase "What happens in Vegas stays in Vegas," sailors and Marines were saying, "What happens in Olongapo stays in Olongapo." Or Hong Kong. Or Amsterdam. Or any number of other ports of call.

It's a hoary cliché, the sailor with a girl in every port. But like all clichés, there's an element of truth to it. Sex and soldiers have gone together for millenniums. Ancient armies moved with an entourage that included an ample number of prostitutes. Illicit sex remains an area of weakness for today's military. And it's not just a problem in overseas posts. The Internet and DVDs bring virtual sex onto stateside military bases, and outside the gates there is the customary commercial strip with "gentlemen's clubs," adult bookstores, massage parlors, and other businesses that trade on illicit sex.

Some will tell you it's harmless. But many of the problems facing society, including the military, can be traced directly to promiscuity and other forms of sexual deviancy. (I use the word *deviancy* not as a caricature of a dirty old man in a trench coat, but in its literal sense: a deviation from the norm as God intended it.)

God did not intend sex to be dirty, furtive, something to be ashamed of. In its proper context, it is meant to mirror our relationship with God. That means it's not just a physical act; it's the beauty of knowing someone on a deep, spiritual level. It's not just

head knowledge—knowing some things *about* the other person—
it's the adventure of truly *knowing* the other person.

THE ONE-FLESH UNION

In the King James Version of the Bible, Genesis 4:1 reads, "Adam
knew Eve his wife; and she conceived." The word *knew* in this context refers to the sex act. (How else could Eve conceive a child?) But
throughout the Bible, the word *know* also means deep, intimate
knowledge—not head knowledge, but heart knowledge. In the
New Testament Jesus says many people know God in a theoretical
sense, in a head-knowledge way, but they never know him spiritually. "Many will say to me on that day, 'Lord, Lord, did we not
prophesy in your name, and in your name drive out demons and
perform many miracles?' Then I will tell them plainly, 'I never
knew you. Away from me, you evildoers!'" (Matthew 7:22–23).
The word *knew* here denotes deep, spiritual, heart knowledge.

Sex as God intends it is to be both physical union—"knowledge" as mentioned in Genesis 4:1—*and* spiritual knowledge of
your spouse's soul. Each reinforces the other. Jesus said, "Haven't
you read...that at the beginning the Creator 'made them male and
female,' and said, 'For this reason a man will leave his father and
mother and be united to his wife, and the two will become one
flesh'? So they are no longer two, but one. Therefore what God has
joined together, let man not separate" (Matthew 19:4–6).

This concept of "one flesh" is crucial to a complete understanding of the biblical view of sex. There is something about the sexual act that brings about a union of two people, *whether or not* they are married to each other. The apostle Paul wrote, "Do you not know that he who unites himself with a prostitute is one with her in body? For it is said, 'The two will become one flesh'" (1 Corinthians 6:16). That helps explain why sex outside of marriage is so damaging. It creates a one-flesh bond that the partners don't intend to be permanent. And while fornication (sex between unmarried people) and adultery (sex when at least one partner is married, but not to the sexual partner) are both condemned in Scripture, adultery is a degree worse because it not only tears apart an existing one-flesh union, but it's a unique act of unfaithfulness. That's why God often refers to idolatry and unbelief as a form of adultery—spiritual unfaithfulness to God (see Matthew 12:39; Mark 8:38).

The one-flesh aspect of sex also helps explain why pornography is so damaging. Since pornography is almost always accompanied by masturbation, it's an attempt to enjoy the pleasurable/physical aspect of a sexual relationship without biblical intimacy, the spiritual/knowledgeable part of righteous sex. Using pornography as a sexual stimulant is an attempt to deny and avoid the biblical truth that sex results in a one-flesh union.

Rachel Zoller, a counselor at Focus on the Family, has an interesting way of looking at this. She says that sex and our perceptions about it are completely intertwined with our beliefs about God. For example, Christianity is about relationship. You start a relationship with God and build on it. As it matures and develops, you have moments of intimacy with him. Then there are times when it seems you're just going through the motions. But the relationship is primary; the intimacy is possible only because you first decided to commit yourself to a relationship with God.

The same ebb and flow is true of marriage. You start the relationship, and the sexual intimacy comes as a result of having first made that unbreakable commitment. The intensity of your sex life will wax and wane, but during a down time you don't worry that you are no longer married. The legitimacy of your marriage and the bond that exists is not based on the intensity of the physical aspect of your relationship. It is established by the covenant of marriage.

The converse is also true, however. Sexual deviancy places the physical aspects above the relationship itself—elevating physical desire and gratification *above* the intimacy of a covenantal relationship. Therefore, when something goes wrong in the physical realm, the partners worry that the whole bond might crumble. In such an upside-down approach to marriage, sex becomes the foundation and the relationship will always be secondary. This is a recipe for disaster, because you can never maintain a constant peak experience in your sex life. The intimacy of your relationship, and the marriage commitment you made that makes intimacy possible, is the basis for everything else that is good about your relationship. Not the other way around.

God's Warnings Against Extramarital Sex

The Bible prohibits sex outside of marriage, but not because God is some sort of cosmic kill-joy. It's because illicit sex is a perversion of the created order. It will destroy you and the relationships that you value most.

> The body is not meant for sexual immorality, but for the Lord, and the Lord for the body.... Flee from sexual immorality. All other sins a man commits are outside his body, but he who sins sexually sins against his own body. (1 Corinthians 6:13, 18)

> Marriage should be honored by all, and the marriage bed kept pure, for God will judge the adulterer and all the sexually immoral. (Hebrews 13:4)

Note here, by the way, that the "marriage bed" can be corrupted even before you're married.

> It is God's will that you should be sanctified: that you should avoid sexual immorality; that each of you should learn to

control his own body in a way that is holy and honorable, not in passionate lust like the heathen, who do not know God;... For God did not call us to be impure, but to live a holy life. Therefore, he who rejects this instruction does not reject man but God. (1 Thessalonians 4:3–5, 7–8)

In addition to the scriptural commands against sexual sin, a host of practical reasons argue against all forms of illicit sex.

1. It threatens your health. Sexual immorality can kill you. Although the U.S. military has a lower incidence of HIV/AIDS than the American population at large, there's always the chance that you'll become one of the statistics. And add into the mix other sexually transmitted diseases (STDs), such as gonorrhea, syphilis, and genital herpes. The latter is incurable and in women can lead to cervical cancer. Today, one in five adults in the United States has an STD, and nineteen million new STD infections occur annually, almost half of them among those of prime military age, eighteen to twenty-four.[1] (I attended a class for naval-gun-fire forward observers at Subic Bay, and out of the fifteen Marines in my class, I was the only one who didn't come down with an STD during the three-week course.)

2. Crimes are associated with sexual immorality. People don't go into the sex trade as a public service. There is almost always a significant criminal connection. One of the

Marines I knew at Subic Bay was robbed when he went home with a "bennie boy"—a transvestite who could easily pass for a beautiful female. The Marine got a rude surprise when he arrived at "her" place, but because the Philippines was under martial law at the time and a midnight curfew was in force, he was stuck with this bennie boy until dawn. Before the Marine was able to leave the next morning, the pimp robbed him of all his money and valuables.

3. Illicit sex funds the modern slave trade. Most of today's human trafficking is connected to the sex trade. The young girls working in brothels and bars, particularly in Southeast Asia, are slaves, bought and sold for others' pleasure. That means to even proposition a prostitute is to condone and finance slave trading. That explains why the military has made it a violation of the Uniform Code of Military Justice to solicit a prostitute. It has also instituted mandatory training about sex-trafficking for units deploying to Africa and Southeast Asia.

4. Pornography destroys lives. Far from being a harmless alternative to actual sex, pornography produces its own set of problems. Whereas it was once thought that porn was a problem only for men, women are increasingly becoming addicted. ChristianityToday.com polled women readers and found that 34 percent admitted to intentionally accessing Internet pornography.[2] In 2004, the *New York*

Times published an article that reported an increasing number of women were viewing online porn,[3] and, according to Nielsen/NetRatings, "nearly one in three visitors to adult Web sites is a woman."[4]

Think about this if you're married: pornography burns images into your mind of sexual partners who are not your spouse. (If you're single but plan to marry, these images are still burned into your memory, often to arise unbidden in the future.) A few years ago at a meeting of the American Academy of Matrimonial Lawyers, two-thirds of the divorce lawyers present said excessive interest in online porn contributed to more than half the divorce cases they handled.[5] Interestingly, pornography played only a tiny role in divorce until the beginning of widespread Internet use, these lawyers reported. That's because in the years prior to the World Wide Web, you had to drive to a seedy part of town and patronize an XXX bookstore or porno theater to gain access to porn, thus having to expose your "secret" in public. But with the Internet, the seedy business enterprise is brought right into your home.

5. Pornography is addictive. A porn habit is akin to being hooked on hard drugs. More than twenty-five years ago, Dr. Victor Cline identified the progressive nature of pornography addiction. Once addicted, a person's need for pornography escalates both in frequency and in deviancy.

The person grows desensitized to the more graphic material, no longer getting a thrill from what once had been exciting.[6] At hearings before the U.S. Senate, medical experts corroborated Cline's early findings. Using technology such as functional magnetic resonance imaging, doctors looked inside addicts' heads to see how their brains reacted to pornography. In many ways, a porn addict's brain responds the same way as a cocaine addict's. Further, because images are stored in the brain and can be recalled at any moment, these experts believe that a porn addiction may be harder to break than a heroin addiction.[7]

6. The number of sex crimes is rising in the military. Sexual assault is a growing problem in the military. It is an issue not only at the service academies, but also aboard ship, in the barracks, and even in units deployed to Iraq and Afghanistan. While there is yet no study establishing a direct, cause-and-effect relationship between sex assaults in the military and the use of porn, the link between pornography and sexual violence has been made elsewhere.[8]

The One Right Choice

With the many scriptural prohibitions of sex outside of marriage and the dangers to your health and safety, the only choice left to the Christian is chastity, meaning sexual faithfulness within marriage and abstinence from sex before marriage. The idea of *chastity* crashes right up against our anything-goes, I-got-my-rights ethos. Still, it is a virtue that can save your life.

C. S. Lewis wrote:

Chastity is the most unpopular of the Christian virtues. There is no getting away from it; the Christian rule is, "Either marriage, with complete faithfulness to your partner, or else total abstinence." Now this is so difficult and so contrary to our instincts that obviously either Christianity is wrong or our sexual instinct, as it now is, has gone wrong. One or the other. Of course, being a Christian, I think it is the instinct which has gone wrong.[9]

Even for the Christian, chastity is hard because of our still-fallen nature—and sometimes the added pressure of well-meaning friends. A retired Air Force officer described how, while on a one-year tour in Korea, local residents helped him find an apartment, complete with a *yobo*, or house girl. The catch was that *yobos* were often much more than maids and cooks. They tended to keep the bed warm at night as well. Only after several polite refusals did the Korean friends figure out that this American liked the apartment but didn't want the *yobo*.

It takes real effort—and teamwork—to fight sexual temptation. One group of Marines preparing to deploy to Thailand prayed that they'd find some Christians there. The Marines prayed every day for a month, and soon they met missionaries through an Internet contact. Once in Thailand, rather than be tempted to visit bars or brothels, they worked with the missionaries at a local orphanage.

Navy chaplain Lieutenant Commander Steve Souders described another visit to Thailand several years ago. The battalion commander, a strong Christian, was so concerned about his young Marines on liberty that he and Souders patrolled the streets in uniform in order to encourage the Marines to keep in line and not break the liberty rules.

"The young girls were hanging out on every street corner," Souders recalled. "As we walked the street we encountered some Marines and sailors who definitely had had too much to drink, while others had a couple of young girls hanging on each arm"—including one Marine who happened to be married. "The CO canceled his liberty on the spot," Souders said. "He ordered him to return to the ship and call his wife so he could be reminded of his commitments back home."

Souders added, "The old saying that what happens overseas stays overseas doesn't work when the Marine or sailor comes home with a venereal disease and passes that little surprise to his wife."

Life Practices That
Promote Sexual Purity

The sex drive is probably the strongest instinct in animals—stronger than even the drive for food. And while humans are certainly "animals" in the sense that our physical bodies function in similar ways and have similar urges, we are much more than animals because we are created in God's image (see Genesis 1:26). We bear the imprint of personhood and possess a moral compass that makes us aware of right and wrong. Sex and marriage are God's creations, and any time we operate outside the way he has set things up, we wind up with nothing but grief.

1. Be aware of your surroundings. Don't undermine your commitment to sexual purity by putting yourself in places and situations where you will be vulnerable to temptation. Avoid bars, strip clubs, certain types of parties, and other venues where immorality is condoned or encouraged. And be aware that you might wind up in such a place by accident. Once, while touring Athens, Greece, I must have left my sixth sense set on "clueless." I found myself not in the restaurant I thought I was visiting, but in a joint where a *very*

aggressive bartender insisted that I buy all the girls a drink. I shot a quick prayer skyward and got out of there as quickly as possible. Lesson learned.

2. Think carefully about whom you spend time with. When you're off duty, avoid people who denigrate sexual purity or demean those who seek to remain faithful to their spouse or fiancée. Also be aware of the people who might represent a personal sexual temptation. You know already which people make a habit of flirting, and those who for whatever reason are especially appealing to you. Know your weaknesses and take steps to remove yourself from tempting situations. Remember, "Bad company corrupts good character" (1 Corinthians 15:33).

3. Be proactive about countering negative influences. Take the initiative against sexual temptation by investing in positive, spiritually healthy relationships and activities. Get involved in ministry or doing volunteer work. Invest your talents and abilities in off-duty activities that are positive, rather than spending your free time in activities that might lead to temptation.

4. Ask a friend to keep you accountable. Your accountability partner could even be a civilian who e-mails you regularly with specific questions. Make sure your accountability partner is someone who will not tolerate excuses or evasive answers. Keep it honest. And look into the various software

programs that automatically send your accountability partner a list of every Web site you visit. You can't indulge in online porn in secret if he's privy to where you've been prowling. (The possibility of getting caught is a much stronger deterrent than Web filters, which are only partially successful.)

5. Get acquainted with your vulnerabilities. Conduct a ruthless self-inventory. Make a list (keep it private) of the people, situations, influences, and places that present a challenge to your commitment to sexual purity. Then avoid behaviors that you know in advance will weaken your resolve. For instance, don't drink to excess and, of course, stay away from all recreational drugs. Always draw the line far in advance of a compromising situation. Rather than going to a bar and flirting with the cocktail waitresses, for example, choose *not* to go to the bar. After all, the object is not to test your willpower by exposing yourself to temptation. And it's not a game to see how close you can get to immorality while still being able to resist sexual contact. That is nothing but foolishness. Wisdom is found in knowing yourself and avoiding the people and places that feed any area of personal weakness. Ask God to strengthen your resolve to avoid those settings, people, and influences.

6. Get smart about seemingly harmless influences. Be aware

of certain television programs, movies, novels, magazines, and other forms of entertainment and diversions that are not rated X, but still can influence you to violate your standards. Avoid any reading matter that glorifies immorality or that arouses your sexual impulses. Even "harmless" material such as the *Sports Illustrated* swimsuit issue, a Victoria's Secret catalog, or an R-rated DVD can wear you down when you are far from home, away from your spouse or fiancée, and feeling lonely and vulnerable.

7. Take advantage of God's Word. Memorize Scripture that encourages sexual purity and biblical morality. Here are a few verses to get you started: 1 Corinthians 6:13, 18; Hebrews 13:4; 1 Thessalonians 4:3–8; 2 Timothy 2:22; Ephesians 5:3.

8. Seek the help of your spouse or fiancée. If you are married or engaged, ask your spouse or fiancée to partner with you to help protect your mental life, emotional life, spiritual life, and sexual life against the ever-present temptations. Prayer support and the support of positive e-mail and other contacts will go far in reminding you of the good thing you have in your marriage or engagement. Remembering how much you value that relationship will help you avoid destroying it through sexual immorality.

9. Don't feed your natural tendency toward disobedience. Part of being a human is that we all have a natural bent

toward disobedience. So retrain your mind toward obedience. Just as in military life you are expected to obey orders immediately, so in the Christian life God expects your full obedience to his commands. "Therefore, I urge you, brothers, in view of God's mercy, to offer your bodies as living sacrifices, holy and pleasing to God—this is your spiritual act of worship. Do not conform any longer to the pattern of this world, but be transformed by the renewing of your mind. Then you will be able to test and approve what God's will is—his good, pleasing and perfect will" (Romans 12:1–2).

"I have been crucified with Christ and I no longer live, but Christ lives in me. The life I live in the body, I live by faith in the Son of God, who loved me and gave himself for me" (Galatians 2:20).

Memorize these verses and meditate on them to help reorient your mind away from sensuality and toward obedience and devotion to God.

7

Protecting the Home Front

How to Avoid the Most Common Marriage Mistakes

[Love] always protects, always trusts,
always hopes, always perseveres.

1 CORINTHIANS 13:7

Wendy Young's husband, Army Captain Chris Young, was home after a yearlong deployment to Iraq. As they ate dinner, Wendy mentioned that a friend, whose husband was currently in Iraq, had been depressed and was losing weight. Cautiously, Wendy mentioned that when Chris was away in 2004, she had gone through a similar experience. A doctor had prescribed antidepressants, but she had turned them down.

This was the first time Chris had heard that his wife had struggled with depression. "I need to know those kinds of things," he said.

"What's the point of telling you?" she replied. "You can't help me fix it."[1]

As much as those words might have hurt Chris Young, they carried extra sting because he was preparing to deploy yet again. If his wife had had those kinds of problems during his first tour of duty but hadn't felt free to communicate them, what would happen now that he was preparing to be away again?

Family life in the military has always come with a set of problems that civilians will never know. Long hours. Long separations. Frequent moves. Loneliness caused by being apart from your spouse and children, and the compounded loneliness of leaving friends behind again and again. Add to the mix the ever-present possibility of death or injury. With our nation at war, those strains are compounded to the point that many military families are near the breaking point.

Today's war on terror is different from past wars: In World Wars I and II and in Korea, the soldiers left home to fight and didn't come back until the war was over—unless they sustained serious injury. In Vietnam, most served a one-year tour and never went back. Today, however, service members face repeated tours overseas, and even when they're "home" they're not home, because they are spending long hours in training to get ready for their next deployment. And for the first time in history, even more so than during the 1991 Gulf War, a large number of wives are serving overseas while their husbands stay home. (And some families have both Mom and Dad deployed.)

Even though danger and death have always been elements of

military service, serving combat duty in a war greatly intensifies the stress factor. Yet according to an informal survey conducted by the Army in February 2005, fear of death or injury is not the leading stress that couples face. The biggest strain on service members and their spouses is the loss of their close relationship as troops face lengthy deployments.[2]

DON'T TRY THIS WITHOUT GOOD COMMUNICATION

A military acronym you might have seen is C^3, sometimes called C-cubed. It stands for command, control, and communication. For today's military families, though, it must stand for communicate, communicate, and communicate.

Here's an example of what can happen when you don't. Army Staff Sergeant Jody Bills's marriage disintegrated midway through his first tour in Iraq, and while many things contributed to the breakup, a lack of *honest* communication was a major factor.[3] Even though he called his wife several times a week, he never told her the full details of what he was doing until, during one call, an incoming mortar round boomed through the phone line. "I am so sick of getting mortared every...day!" he said.

"What do you mean?" his then-wife asked. "I thought you were safe on the base...What's going on?"

That phone call was the first time she realized the nature of what her husband was doing in Iraq. It's understandable that he would want to spare her the worst details, and many find it diffi-cult to talk about such things to begin with. But suddenly finding out the true danger that Jody Bills was facing came as a horrible shock to his wife. As for her part, simply watching the evening news would have given her some idea. Whatever the full reasons, their lack of open communication contributed to the breakup of their marriage.

How to Make the Best of a New Assignment

Anyone who enters the military knows to expect long separations from loved ones. But being aware of this and dealing with the real-ity of a new deployment are two very different things. When you are about to be separated by a new assignment, you can take delib-erate steps ahead of time to make the separation easier to deal with. Here are a few suggestions to help keep both of you connected while you're apart.

1. When you receive new orders for deployment, sit down together and talk about your upcoming separation. As you discuss this, make sure you include what each of you thinks about the coming separation and how you both feel about it. In fact, this needs to be an ongoing conver-sation. As you talk, don't try to hide your anxieties, fears, or frustrations. Things left unsaid—or only suspected by one party or the other—will fester over time.

2. Talk about everything—even the hardest topics. Serving in
the military is never safe, even outside a war zone. Military
members are lost to training accidents, vehicle accidents,
equipment failure or malfunction, and other circumstances.
Studies have shown that families that discuss the possibility
of death in advance adjust better to the loss.[4] Most important, make sure your children are in the communication
loop. Older kids should be included in the conversation.
For younger kids, you need to decide in advance what you
will tell them if Mom or Dad is killed or injured. Only
parents can judge the maturity of their children and decide
when to bring them into the conversation. But generally
speaking, children younger than ten are less able to process
abstract what-ifs in advance. (For them, even trying to grasp
the length of an upcoming deployment can be hard. It's
better to simply state that Mommy or Daddy has to go
away for a period of time—without being too specific.) At
some point you should include a trusted family friend, a
military chaplain, or a pastor in these discussions—especially
for children. They must have spiritual assurances in advance
that despite the separation and the danger involved, God is
in control. If you postpone the "God talk" until after Mom
or Dad has been injured or killed, it will make God seem
like an afterthought and not the source of strength that
your family needs.

3. Keep God at the center of your marriage and family life. If he is not currently occupying that spot, make sure you put him there. You, your spouse, and your children need a vibrant, ongoing relationship with God *before* a deployment. You need to be depending on him *now* for peace, guidance, wisdom, and strength.

4. Have a plan in place in case of emergency. Not everything that can go wrong will involve death or injury—and threats to your family's well-being won't always happen to the soldier. The spouse at home could be in an accident. The house could burn down. In such cases, the Red Cross, your church, friends, and a base Family Readiness group can all be a great help. As a couple, you need to talk *in advance* about how you will make use of the resources that are available.

5. Create a family plan that addresses each family member. As you work out your plan, clearly identify how each of you will manage your time apart. At first the loneliness on both ends will seem crushing. Believe it or not, so will the boredom. (Yes, life in a war zone can consist of long periods of having nothing to do.)

At home, try to maintain as much of a routine as possible. Maintain the same social network as before, especially with your church. An important factor for children is maintaining a sense of normalcy. For this reason, it's probably not a good idea to move to your parents' or in-laws' house. As friendly as those arrangements might be, they're not "normal" for kids. A short vacation at Gram and Gramps' is fine, but if at all possible maintain your same residence during a deployment. Most important, this also keeps you connected to your normal social network.

For both spouses, be aware of the temptation to turn to drugs or alcohol to ease the pain. If you isolate yourself from your community, this becomes even more dangerous. Turning to drugs or alcohol often are early signs that you're trying to self-medicate a bout with depression. If you feel you need something to dull your pain, that's a signal that you need to talk to a chaplain, pastor, or doctor.

6. Prepare a comm plan in advance. Depending on where Mom or Dad will be deployed, families may have regular e-mail contact and occasional telephone contact. Even submarines now have the ability to transmit e-mail via burst transmission. But even with all this technology, there are some things you will still want to ship overseas. Send voice recordings on CD, home movies on DVD, and other goodies via a care package. And don't forget good old pen and paper. There is nothing as sweet as the smell of a letter from home.

As part of your comm plan, talk about realistic expectations. I have talked to the spouses of enlisted personnel who were hurt because they were not getting regular phone calls. Telephone calls are glorious, yet expensive, so plan for them in your budget.

7. Keep things as upbeat as possible—but be honest. If there is a problem at home or with the kids that the deployed spouse can do little about, there's not much point in dwelling on it. But that doesn't mean you shouldn't keep your spouse apprised of day-to-day developments at home. Keep him in the loop regarding kids, friends, work, and your day-to-day life. As for the deployed spouse, be patient and understand the need to communicate. Be sure to ask your mate about his or her ordinary life experiences and events. The deployed spouse also has to be as straightforward as possible. That does not mean you have to give all the gory details; it does mean you should not lie by omission, giving a false sense of security if it's not warranted. And if you are facing a crisis, but it's impossible for your mate to do anything to help, then let her know what's going on, but also make it clear how you are handling it.

Life Practices That
Smooth Your Return Home

Even though deployments can seem endless, at some point your soldier will be coming home. As the return date nears, anticipation builds. And therein lies a potential danger, because all that time of loneliness and longing can set up unrealistic expectations. The soldier looks forward to a chance to return to normal life, marital intimacy, and real food. In addition, the kids look forward to Dad or Mom being back home.

Mixed in with the excitement of the return are concerns about how the reunion will go. The truth is that everything and everyone will have changed, some more than others. You can never go back to things exactly as they were before, and wishing to do so only sets you up for disappointment. The reunion will be amazing, but daily life goes on. The dishes still need to be washed and the lawn mowed. One soldier described how wonderful it was to see his wife wearing a sexy dress. A wonderful afternoon and evening of lovemaking came to an end the next morning when his two-year-old welcomed him home with projectile vomiting and diarrhea. *That* was a reality check.

When you are separated by a new assignment or long-term

deployment, you can't wait to be together again. Finally the day arrives, and you are both overjoyed. And then comes the adjustment. Reconnecting, for all the joy it involves, also presents a real challenge. So remember one thing: communication is paramount. Here are a few suggestions to help keep both of you open with each other—and talking—as you learn how to live together again.

1. Stay loose, and know your backup plan. Remember, military flights sometimes run on their own schedule. After seven years in the Marine Corps, I adapted its motto to the reality of military life: Semper Gumby (Always Flexible).

2. Your spouse and kids will have changed. Do your best to say only positive things. In fact, go out of your way to look for good things to say about your spouse, the kids, and the house. Save any questions or criticisms until after life has returned to some sense of normalcy. Don't immediately try to change things back to the way they were. John Thurman, an Army Reserve chaplain, said this required a major adjustment on his part. "I was amazed at how well my wife and kids had done," he said. "I let myself feel hurt, and that was not too bright." His advice: focus on how proud you are of all they accomplished while you were away.

3. Plan a special celebration. Do it up big with banners, favorite foods, and a party with as many friends and family members present as possible. But be smart about the timing.

Remember that your returning hero likely will be tired, distracted, busy, or anxious upon arrival. He or she may not have slept for a day or more. The soldier will most likely want to chill for a few days, so don't make too many big plans for the first few days home.

4. Reintroduce yourselves. Once life starts to return to normal, don't be surprised if you both feel like strangers. This is normal after a long deployment, so make your spouse and kids your first priority. And realize that at first your kids will test the rules. So be sure to brief your soldier spouse (in private) on any rule changes that happened during the deployment. This way you can present a united front.

5. Plan time alone to talk and reconnect. Chuck Milligan, a graduate of the Air Force Academy who served twenty years before retiring, described how he and his wife, Annette, handled their reunions. "Our solution has been to try to make time to see each other for a short while before meeting with the whole family," he said. "Even if it's just the drive home from the airport, it's something. Toward the end of my remote tour to Korea, Annette flew out for a couple of weeks before I came back. My folks watched the kids, and we got a chance to reacquaint. It was great, because I was ready to be with the kids when we got back together. Annette was a hero to the girls as well, since she told them she 'found' me and brought me to them."

6. Factor in other friendships, especially within the military. Remember, the soldier has just spent a long time under a lot of stress with his buddies. Don't feel hurt or insulted if he wants to reconnect with them. The bonds forged in wartime are incredibly strong. In 2 Samuel 1:26, Israel's King David grieves the death of his beloved friend. "I grieve for you, Jonathan my brother; you were very dear to me. Your love for me was wonderful, more wonderful than that of women."

7. Be patient with sex. Sexual relations and intimacy may be challenging at first. Try to remember how it was when you were first married, when things were new and adjustments were needed. It will take time and patience to get reacquainted and to feel completely comfortable with each other. Women, if need be, talk to your doctor about any concerns.

8. Grant both spouses equal rank. If by day you lead a large number of people, remember that at home your spouse is not under your direct command. It can be hard to break out of command mode into spouse and parent mode. For the wives or husbands, be understanding. For the soldier, listen to how you're speaking to your wife or children. It has been more than twenty-five years since I wore a Marine uniform, yet my son still complains that sometimes I talk to him in my "Marine voice." Old habits die

hard—or hardly, in my case.

9. For family members: respect a legitimate need for privacy. Don't force the returning soldier (your spouse or parent) to talk about what he or she experienced on deployment, especially if it was in a combat zone. He needs time to process this information himself. And in fact, he may never want to talk about it. My father fought in Europe in World War II, and to this day I don't fully know what he did. The few times I pressed him for information, he found a way to change the subject. This is not unusual. We're all familiar with the famous photo of the Marines raising the American flag at Iwo Jima. But James Bradley did not know that his father was one of those six men until his dad died in 1994. His father had seen no need to mention it—or possibly he couldn't raise the subject lest it bring back memories he didn't want to talk about. Personally, I believe it was the latter.[5]

Accept that you may never fully learn what your soldier saw and did while in a war zone. At the same time, be ready to listen when he decides to talk. Chances are this won't be a planned event; it will be spontaneous. When it happens, listen without judging. If he seems particularly distressed and unable to get over something, gently suggest he seek counseling or that he talk with a chaplain.

10. Learn to adjust to changes in the life of the veteran. What

if your spouse comes home wounded, possibly with a permanent disability? All the normal coming-home difficulties are compounded. "The young stud that the woman married, when he comes back injured, is no longer a stud," said one Army counselor. This is where the strength of the relationship before the deployment will play a key role.

Army Sergeant Joseph Bozik lost both legs and part of an arm to an explosion in Iraq. He and his girlfriend, Jayme Peters, had talked of getting married before he was deployed, but as he recuperated at Walter Reed Army Medical Center, he felt he could no longer hold her to the commitment. "Be completely honest with me," he told Jayme. "If you want to go home, that's fine."

She started to cry. "I knew that he was eventually going to tell me that I could go," she recalled. "He was just that kind of guy." And that pained her, she said, because she didn't want him to doubt her even for a moment.

"I told him that I loved him," she said. "I was willing to be with him the rest of my life if he would let me."

They were married December 31, 2004, in a hospital chapel.[6]

11. Rely on God and your faith. Even in extreme circumstances, God is present and available to help you. Consider the case of Dave Roever, a Vietnam veteran who had a strong Christian background to rely on as he recuperated

from his war wounds, and later, as his wife had to adjust to a husband with serious injuries.

Roever, a member of a Navy river attack boat in the Mekong Delta, was severely burned when a bullet struck the incendiary grenade he was about to throw. As he lay in his bed in a hospital burn ward, he saw another man's wife come in. She looked at her dying husband's charred body and said, "You're embarrassing. I couldn't walk down the street with you." Dave watched the woman leave her wedding ring on the bed and walk away. For Dave, imagined images of his own wife crying out in disgust haunted him. So when Brenda walked in, he braced himself for such a reaction. But instead, she kissed his severely burned and deformed face and told him that she took their marriage vows seriously; she would never leave him.[7]

From the time of Adam and Eve, the first married couple, God has made it clear that marriage is not an "army of one." Instead, it is two people who have become one flesh (see Genesis 2:24). Because you and your spouse are one in marriage, when long distances separate you, you can't help but feel that a part of you is missing. That explains, in part, why military life can be such a lonely life.

You wish you could be spending time with your mate and

children. You long for their hugs, and you deeply miss the intimacy of sex with your spouse. Friendships and camaraderie are important, but they can't fill the void that is created when your family is home while you are serving overseas. And all of these longings make reuniting after a long deployment a bigger challenge than you think it will be.

Whether you are being deployed or about to return home, use the practical suggestions in this chapter to help you deal with loneliness and, upon your return, to help your reunion go as smoothly as possible.

8

What to Do with Your Anger

How to Put Vengeance Back into God's Hands

In your anger do not sin: Do not let the
sun go down while you are still angry.

EPHESIANS 4:26

The time was 7:49 a.m., December 7, 1941. Commander Mitsuo Fuchida was admiring the billowing clouds and brilliant sunrise as he led a squadron of 360 Japanese fighters, bombers, and torpedo planes over the Hawaiian island of Oahu. Just four days after his thirty-ninth birthday, Fuchida was in charge of a bold gamble by imperial Japan: knock out the U.S. Pacific Fleet in one crushing blow, which would give Japan free rein to continue its conquest of Asia and the Pacific.

Seeing the fleet sitting peacefully at anchor three thousand meters below, Fuchida smiled as he ordered, "All squadrons, plunge in to attack!" He then radioed back to the Japanese fleet

230 miles away: *"Tora, tora, tora!"* The attack had begun![1]

What followed was, in the words of President Franklin Roosevelt, "a day which will live in infamy." Of eight battleships in the harbor, five were destroyed. Fourteen other ships were sunk or damaged. More than 2,300 Americans lay dead or dying, many trapped within the hulls of their sinking ships. Fuchida later described the day as "the most thrilling exploit of my career."

At that same time, Sergeant Jacob DeShazer of the U.S. Army Air Corps was on KP duty, peeling potatoes at his base in Oregon. Upon hearing the news over the radio, DeShazer hurled a potato against the wall, screaming, "The Japs are going to have to pay for this!"[2]

Anger. It's the normal human reaction to a wrong that has been committed, either against you or someone else. It's a natural human emotion. In fact, the words *anger* and *angry* appear more than 350 times in the Bible, many times referring to God's anger. And since we are created in his image, it makes sense that we share this reaction to injustice and wrong.

DeShazer's reaction to the sneak attack on Pearl Harbor was perfectly understandable and even justified. When your own guys are killed in an unprovoked attack, the injustice of the situation gives rise to anger. There's a difference, though, between human anger and God's wrath. God's anger is always righteous. And it takes a lot to get him angry. "The LORD is slow to anger, abounding in love and forgiving sin and rebellion" (Numbers 14:18). But with us humans…well, let's just say our anger is not always righteous, and some of us get teed off pretty easily. In the case of Jake DeShazer, his initial righteous anger quickly degenerated into hatred, and it almost led to his death. But God was able to redeem that anger and use it for good. (More on that in a bit.)

ANGER IN WAR

Anger has found its place on the battlefield ever since there have been battles. The ancients understood that in certain circumstances anger is appropriate—and indeed pleasant. (In ancient Greek the word for anger, *thumos,* is also translated as spiritedness.) Perhaps one of the more famous examples of battlefield anger can be found in Homer's *Iliad.* The Greeks had been besieging Troy for years when Achilles' beloved friend, Patroclus, is killed by the Trojan hero, Hector. At first Achilles sulks, but then he lets his anger cross a line into a thirst for vengeance: "I will not live nor go about among mankind unless Hector fall by my spear, and thus pay me for having slain Patroclus."[3]

Achilles, regretting that anger has disturbed his judgment, speaks of that anger "wherein even a righteous man will harden his heart—which rises up in the soul of a man like smoke, and the taste thereof is sweeter than drops of honey."[4]

THE ANGER OF VENGEANCE

The Bible is familiar with anger, both the righteous variety and the vengeful distortion. One of the more disturbing passages of Scripture is Psalm 137:8–9, a so-called imprecatory (cursing) psalm. The writer, in his anger at Babylon's captivity of God's people, looks forward to the city's judgment: "O Daughter of Babylon, doomed to destruction, happy is he who repays you for what you have done to us—he who seizes your infants and dashes them against the rocks."

Anger can be like a sore tooth. It hurts, but somehow there is a perverse pleasure in pushing your tongue against it to test the pain. Left to fester, however, the infection will spread and multiply its destruction. Nursing your anger is like letting an infection wreak havoc in your body. And if left unaddressed, it will lead you to do things you otherwise wouldn't do.

Achilles, a skilled warrior who normally honored the enemy dead, went into a berserk state after the death of Patroclus, which led him to acts of barbarism. Not merely satisfied with killing Hector in revenge, Achilles mutilates and degrades Hector's body by hooking it to a chariot and dragging it around Patroclus's tomb. And even that was not enough. As Homer writes, "Thus shamefully did Achilles in his fury dishonour Hector [for twelve days]."[5]

ANGER ON THE BATTLEFIELD

A Marine veteran of Vietnam describes his own anger and explains how by feeding his anger it eventually grew into rage:

> I built up such hate. I couldn't do enough damage. Got worse as time went by. I really loved [expletive] killing. Couldn't get enough. For every one that I killed, I felt better. Made some of the hurt go away. Every time you lost a friend, it seemed like a part of you was gone. Get one of them to compensate for what they had done to me. I got very hard, cold, merciless. I lost all mercy.[6]

A former Army Ranger speaks of an incident in Iraq when anger nearly led to the death of a little girl. His unit had just taken small-arms fire and mortar rounds from an unseen enemy. "We began to return fire without confirming our targets," the soldier said, as the heat of the moment got the better of their training and their judgment. Between the soldiers and the enemy was a little girl wearing a head scarf. "We were mostly firing beyond her and over her head, but some of the guys saw her and thought she was a man wearing a black hood, which is not uncommon for insurgents to wear."

Realizing it was a little girl, this Ranger gave the hand-and-arm signal to cease fire, and the little girl began to run away. "I began to run after her," he says. "My wisdom had lapsed, and my discernment was poor. The terrified thing ran away across a field, ripping off her head scarf to show us her long brown-and-gold hair to expose herself as not being a threat. I ran after her in an attempt to apologize and comfort her and tell her that we were sorry. I wanted to catch her, not just for her sake, but for my own. But she made it to the family vehicle before I could catch her and they sped away."

He looks back at that moment with regret. "That was my lowest time," he said. "It conjured the most anger—and it was at myself. That night my prayers were for forgiveness."

Of course, it does not take a battle to make a soldier angry. Lieutenant Adam Morehouse, who served in Iraq with the 2nd Infantry Division, said he saw soldiers become angry even at Iraqis who were *not* fighting them. "We perceived an ingratitude on their part," Morehouse said. "We saw an apparent unwillingness to stand up for themselves, their families, their land."

Some of the anger grew out of cultural differences. "The Arabs are fatalistic," he explained. If something bad is happening to them, they see it as God's will. (That's why Arabs will often say, *"Ins'allah"*—if God wills it.) "We saw it as an excuse for not acting," Morehouse added. "A lot of the guys developed prejudices against Arabs in general and Iraqis in particular. There were incidents when I had to stand up when someone wasn't treating civilians right. I had to step up and tell them how to behave...I was in a unique situation as a Christian."

Prejudice rises to the surface in the opposite direction as well. For instance, when serving overseas, cultural differences can affect the way U.S. military personnel are treated based on their gender. In Iraq, one of Captain Krista Jekielek's jobs was to develop a logistics system for the Iraqi army, which meant frequent contact with Arab men. "It's hard to deal with the Iraqi soldiers because I am a woman," she said. "I have been pushed to the side and yelled at by plenty of Iraqi generals and Iraqi contractors." She didn't let the demeaning behavior get to her, though. "I kept it professional, but it was frustrating because our views are so different."

ANGER THAT IS RIGHTEOUS

Righteous anger honors God; vengeful anger dishonors God and often leads to sin. God's anger is *always* properly directed toward a wrong. God expresses his anger, not to make himself feel better, but to judge evil. How many of us can say the same thing?

The Bible does *not* tell us not to get angry, though. Anger is sometimes justified, and it must be properly expressed. As the apostle Paul wrote, "'In your anger do not sin': Do not let the sun go down while you are still angry, and do not give the devil a foothold" (Ephesians 4:26–27). If you let your anger fester, you open yourself to sin. It can evidence itself in prejudice, as Lieutenant Morehouse describes. At its worst, it can turn into open hatred and murderous rage, as attested to by the Vietnam veteran quoted earlier.

If we rely on our own strength to control our anger, we only make things harder. And, in fact, we set ourselves up for failure. In the end the battle is the Lord's (see 1 Samuel 17:47). If you are angered at evil, know that "The LORD is a jealous and avenging God; the LORD takes vengeance and is filled with wrath. The LORD takes vengeance on his foes and maintains his wrath against his enemies" (Nahum 1:2). God's wrath is not anger for the sake of venting frustration, nor is it spite or verbal castigation. God's wrath is righteous judgment rendered by the Ultimate Judge.

THE ATTACK ON PEARL HARBOR

You might be wondering what happened to Sergeant DeShazer, the soldier peeling potatoes in Oregon when the Japanese attacked Pearl Harbor. He got angry at the treachery, and rightly so. It's where he let the anger take him that became a problem. He let it fester into hatred. DeShazer said the "Japs" would have to pay for their treachery, and he was good to his word. He volunteered to join a special squadron being formed by Lieutenant Colonel Jimmy Doolittle, whose mission was to take the war directly to the Japanese in a daring bombing raid over Tokyo.

It was an audacious plan. Sixteen highly modified B-25 Mitchell bombers would take off from an aircraft carrier, the USS Hornet, and bomb the Japanese homeland, then fly to allied bases in China. B-25s were not designed to take off from the deck of an aircraft carrier, nor were carriers designed for something as big and lumbering as the B-25 bomber. On the morning of April 18, 1942, still about 650 miles from Japan, the Hornet was sighted by a Japanese picket boat, which radioed an attack warning back to headquarters. Because of this, Doolittle decided to launch the raid a day early and about two hundred miles farther from Japan than planned. Despite the fact that none of the B-25 pilots, including Doolittle, had ever taken off from a carrier before, all sixteen planes took off safely. The pilots flew single file toward Japan at wave-top level to avoid detection. They arrived over Japan about noon and bombed military targets in Tokyo, Yokohama, Kobe, Osaka, and Nagoya.

Militarily, the Doolittle Raid was only a pinprick. As a morale booster for Americans, though, it was a stunning success. But because the raiders had been forced to launch early, several of the bombers began to run low on fuel before they made it all the way to the airfields in China. Still, most made it to safety, although two planes and their crews were unaccounted for. One of them was DeShazer's.

He would spend the next forty months as a prisoner of Japan, thirty-four of those months in solitary confinement, during which he was routinely tortured. His burning hatred of the Japanese was fanned into an inferno. As fellow American prisoners were executed or died of starvation, disease, or torture, DeShazer remained alive—if barely.

His solitary confinement gave him time to ponder the human condition. He wondered what could cause such hatred among humans. Barely remembering Sunday school lessons from childhood, he asked his Japanese guards for a Bible. Two years after his capture he finally received one and eagerly read it, learning lessons about mercy, forgiveness, and redemption. He later wrote, "I discovered that God had given me new spiritual eyes and that when I looked at the enemy officers and guards who had starved and beaten my companions and me so cruelly, I found my bitter hatred for them changed to loving pity.... I prayed for God to forgive my torturers, and I determined by the aid of Christ to do my best to acquaint these people with the message of salvation."

On August 20, 1945, a smiling Japanese guard swung open DeShazer's cell door and said, "War over. You go home now."[7]

DeShazer wrote a book called *I Was a Prisoner of Japan* and, after studying at what was then Seattle Pacific College, returned to Japan, this time as a missionary to his former enemies. Fuchida, in the meantime, tried to return to a life of farming. But deeply shamed by Japan's loss and still with the heart of a warrior, it was an unsatisfying life. Even though married, he had a mistress in Tokyo and made many excuses to his wife, Haruko, for why he had to travel there frequently.

One day in October 1948, while getting off a train in Tokyo, Fuchida saw an American handing out leaflets printed in Japanese. The title caught his eye: *Watakushi Wa Nippon No Horyo Deshita* (I Was a Prisoner of Japan). It grabbed his attention immediately, especially since it started out talking about Pearl Harbor. Fuchida determined to learn more about this man, not out of any interest in Christianity, but because he wanted to know more about Jake DeShazer. Even though they had been enemies in the war, Fuchida had admired the courage of the Doolittle Raiders.

He was taken with DeShazer's Christian testimony, too. A friend told him to get a Bible, but Fuchida could not find one written in Japanese. Then, on a train platform, he noticed a Japanese man with boxes of books: "Get your Bible—food for your soul," the man cried in Japanese. Struck by the coincidence and despite his Shinto heritage, Fuchida bought one for forty yen, a pittance at the time. He was struck by Jesus' words in Luke 23:34, "Father, forgive them, for they do not know what they are doing."

Later Fuchida wrote: "I was impressed that I was certainly one of those for whom Jesus had prayed. The many men I had killed had been slaughtered in the name of patriotism, for I did not understand the love of Christ."[8] He changed from a bitter ex-war hero to a man on a new mission. He went on to become an evangelist throughout Japan and Asia, and he and Jake DeShazer eventually became close friends.

Fuchida died in 1976 at the age of seventy-four. DeShazer today is in his eighties and lives with his wife, Florence, in Salem, Oregon. More than six decades ago, the two men were bitter enemies. But in their old age they were brothers, a testimony to the power of God's grace—and his power to turn away anger.

Life Practices That
Minimize Destructive Anger

Anger is like money: it can serve a noble purpose or it can bring about greater evil. Righteous anger energizes you to take needed action against injustice; unrighteous anger inflames your emotions and pushes you to add greater suffering and destructiveness to an already-bad situation. God gave you free will, so you have the power to decide what you will do with your anger. The following tips will help you differentiate between righteous anger and anger that will lead only to greater harm.

1. Don't get real angry; get real about anger. It's easy to think we are punishing others through our anger, that our anger toward them will "teach them a lesson." In truth, the person who is hurt most by your anger is you and, all too often, those closest to you. When you are seething inside, you are likely to take it out on your spouse, your children, and your friends. So get real about your anger; notice who is really victimized by your rage.

2. Understand the biblical purpose of anger. Read the story of Jesus clearing the money changers out of the

temple (see Matthew 21:12–13; Mark 11:15–18; John 2:14–17). Jesus' ire was aroused because unscrupulous merchants were taking advantage of worshippers who came to the temple to offer sacrifices. Through their unethical practices, the merchants were turning God's house of prayer into "a den of robbers" (Mark 11:17). Jesus took action against a wrong; his anger was kindled against injustice. That is a vivid picture of the biblical purpose of righteous anger—it's a call to action against evil. The next time you get angry, measure your anger against this biblical yardstick.

3. Investigate what's underneath your anger. Anger is often the outward manifestation of a different, deeper emotion. So take a look inside to see what lies beneath your anger. Have you lost a friend in battle, and your anger is covering your grief and sorrow? Are you worried about a family member back home who is struggling with illness—or suffering in some other way—and you feel helpless in the face of your loved one's need? Does your role in the military put you in a pressure cooker environment day after day, producing stress and frustration that are expressed in anger? Ask God to show you what is behind your anger.

4. Notice the effect of anger in your life. We like to believe that anger moves outward, to wreak havoc in the lives of evildoers. But most often, it seeps inward, poisoning the

life of the person who generates and expresses the anger. The effects can range from high blood pressure, headaches, and indigestion to other effects such as insomnia, difficulty concentrating, and depression. Deal with your anger so that it doesn't destroy you.

5. Ask a trusted friend to help gauge your anger. None of us is objective about our own behavior, habits, and weaknesses. But a friend who knows you well and who is committed to what is best for you can help you see yourself as you really are. Take a friend into your confidence, and tell him or her that you are committed to dealing with your anger. Ask your friend to let you know when your anger is unjustified and when it is used to belittle, demean, or lash out. When your friend gives you feedback, listen carefully and avoid the urge to defend yourself.

6. Take responsibility for how you react. You are not at the mercy of your anger. The only one who can control your reactions is you. Ultimately, people and circumstances have no power over your emotions; you exercise control over yourself and your responses. It's a myth, for instance, that someone can make you angry, fearful, sad, or depressed. While the words and actions of others do elicit feelings and reactions in you, you have the power to control how you react. "You make me so angry!" is what it might feel like. But the truth is, you choose to get angry in

response to the words and actions of others. Conversely, you can choose not to get angry. It's up to you.

7. Commit your anger to prayer. No matter how self-disciplined you are, you'll need help if you are ever to get your anger under control. In saying that, I'm not judging you or suggesting that you are weaker than other people. We are all weak, and without God's help we can't accomplish much in life. When it comes to a destructive force such as anger, we all need help. So ask God to help you identify the causes of your anger and to help you control it. Jesus instructed us: "Ask and it will be given to you; seek and you will find; knock and the door will be opened to you" (Matthew 7:7). Ask God to help you rid your life of the destruction of unrighteous anger.

9

★★★★

Getting Answers About Grief

How to Handle the Pain of Loss

"Where have you laid him?" he [Jesus]
asked. "Come and see, Lord," they
replied. Jesus wept.

JOHN 11:34–35

★★★★

Honor, bravery, duty. All were in abundance in Mogadishu, Somalia, during a mission in 1993. The mission—planned as a forty-five-minute "snatch and grab" operation—ended in disaster and was immortalized in the book and movie *Black Hawk Down*. The date October 3, 1993, has gone down in history as a black day for the United States Army.

In the failed mission, designed to capture key lieutenants of Somali warlord Mohamed Farrah Aidid, two Black Hawk helicopters were shot down over downtown Mogadishu. The operation suddenly turned into a desperate rescue mission—in the heart of Aidid's personal fiefdom—as additional units were sent in to rescue soldiers trapped by rampaging, heavily armed mobs. The Americans were quickly besieged, and what followed is a story of incredible selflessness and bravery.

Army Rangers and Delta Force soldiers found themselves trapped in a situation they were ill-equipped to deal with—a fifteen-hour ordeal that left eighteen Americans dead and dozens wounded, not to mention the estimated one thousand Somalis killed.

Lieutenant General William "Jerry" Boykin, a colonel at the time, commanded the Delta Force. After the battle, he stood near a hangar at the Mogadishu airport as a five-ton truck brought back the bodies of the soldiers killed during the battle. "They dropped the tailgate and blood poured out like water," he remembered. "I was absolutely devastated. Those were my soldiers. I was in disbelief that God would allow something like this."

Things would get worse. Nearby was one of the Humvees used in the rescue mission. Inside, blood and brain matter were splattered all over the vehicle's interior. A few hours later Boykin saw a captured American pilot, Warrant Officer Mike Durant, on a small black-and-white TV screen. And then came the worst sight of all—televised images of naked and mutilated American bodies being dragged through the streets of Mogadishu as mobs celebrated.

"I was already numb," Boykin said. "This was beyond a night-mare. *I must be dreaming*, I thought. My mind could not accept that, having depended on God, this could happen."

At first he had no time to mourn. "I still had ops to run through that day," he said. "I had to get a head count, figure out who was hurt, who was missing." Later he went to a makeshift morgue to ID the dead soldiers. "I unzipped body bags and looked into ashen faces of my men. I thought, *Am I responsible? Did I train this soldier properly? Did I lead him properly? Did I do everything to ensure this soldier survived?*"

Doubt and guilt ate at Jerry Boykin. That night, he collapsed onto his bed and started crying. "It was the first time I could release my emotions."

THE FACES OF GRIEF

Grief shows itself in many ways. Fear. Anger. And, mostly, *pain.* But also numbness and doubt.

C. S. Lewis suffered intense grief when his wife, Joy, died. Through his pain, he was able to stand back and observe the process of grieving:

> No one ever told me that grief felt so like fear. I am not afraid, but the sensation is like being afraid. The same fluttering in the stomach, the same restlessness, the yawning. I keep swallowing.
>
> At other times it feels like being mildly drunk, or

concussed. There is a sort of invisible blanket between the world and me. I find it hard to take in what anyone says.[1]

Different cultures express grief in different ways. A frequent response in the Bible is to abase oneself, to rend one's clothing and to roll around in the dirt: "O my people, put on sackcloth and roll in ashes; mourn with bitter wailing as for an only son, for suddenly the destroyer will come upon us" (Jeremiah 6:26).

Compare this to other ancient practices. As he did with anger, Homer captures the experience of grief in describing Achilles' reaction to the death of his beloved friend, Patroclus.

"A dark cloud of grief fell upon Achilles.... He filled both hands with dust from off the ground, and poured it over his head, disfiguring his comely face, and letting the refuse settle over his shirt so fair and new. He flung himself down all huge and hugely at full length, and tore his hair with his hands."[2]

Grief Is Not Weakness

Even today, it is common for those in the Middle East to grieve with extreme wailing and emotion. That's not necessarily a bad thing, either. Unfortunately, in our Western culture and particularly in the military culture overt grief has been frowned upon.

"An American soldier who wept for a fallen friend was warned not to 'lose it' and to 'get your mind straight,'" writes Dr. Jonathan Shay. "One man, holding a dead friend, was told, 'Stuff those tears!' and 'Don't get mad, get even' by his company commander.... American military culture in Vietnam regarded tears as dangerous but above all as demeaning, the sign of a weakling, a loser. To weep was to lose one's dignity among American soldiers in Vietnam."[3]

Grief Is Not a Lack of Faith

Unfortunately, among some Christians, an overt expression of grief is seen as a lack of faith. Nothing could be further from the truth. When I was in high school I attended a church youth group meeting. A young woman from the group had just lost a long battle with cancer, and even though I didn't know her, I was struck by the tragedy of her dying at such a young age. But one of the youth leaders' responses to the news puzzled—no, shocked—me: "Praise the Lord!" he said.

Huh?! I didn't know much about Christianity at the time, but looking back I can understand what the well-meaning but misguided man was *trying* to say. The young girl had trusted the Lord with her salvation, so we realized she was now with the Lord (see 2 Corinthians 5:6–8). But, on the other hand, she was *dead!* Her family and friends were loaded down with sorrow over losing this precious girl. Shouldn't we all share in their grief? The answer was yes.

Grief is the natural human response to severe loss. We have the example of the Lord himself. When he learned that his friend

Lazarus had died, Jesus wept (see John 11:35). Think about this: the Lord of the universe, the man with the power of life in his hands, cried at the death of a friend. This is even more remarkable when you consider that Jesus already knew that the death of his friend was not permanent. In a few moments he was going to raise Lazarus from the grave (see John 11:43–44).

It is not a denial of your faith to grieve. The psalms are full of weeping and sorrow. An entire book of the Bible is called Lamentations. In the New Testament, after Stephen had been stoned to death (see Acts 7:55–60), we're told that "Godly men buried Stephen and mourned deeply for him" (Acts 8:2). Even these men, who had so recently witnessed the living Christ after his resurrection, grieved the death of a friend. In Romans 12:15, we're told to mourn with those who mourn. We are commanded to come alongside the sorrowful. Likewise, when we are grieving, others are told to offer us comfort and support.

Grief Is Mitigated by Hope

We know that our mourning is not the end. After all, we are not to "grieve like the rest of men, who have no hope" (1 Thessalonians 4:13). We have the hope of resurrection and eternal life. We can pour out our pain to God, knowing that ultimately he is in control of all that happens. In Psalm 62:8 David instructed, "O people; pour out your hearts to him, for God is our refuge." God can handle our raw emotions, even when we cry out in anger, doubt, and pain. He understands our grief and the confusion and suffering that go along with it.

Sometimes we grieve not only because we have lost a friend, but also because of the timing and the way the death occurred. Captain Krista Jekielek, a logistics officer with the 1st Brigade Combat Team, was supervising Iraqi contract workers as they closed down a forward operating base in Northern Iraq. "Our convoy was hit by an IED," she explains. "Sagueen was hit in his femoral artery and bled out. I took personal responsibility for his death. I had yelled at him the day before and never had time to apologize. That experience made me realize how important it is to act like a Christian. We may never have time to say we're sorry. It wasn't fair. Death never is."

Perhaps the hardest thing about losing someone is wondering why God would allow such a senseless loss. As C. S. Lewis wrote,

"Meanwhile, where is God? This is one of the most disquieting symptoms. When you are happy, so happy that you have no sense of needing him,...you will be—or so it feels— welcomed with open arms. But go to him when your need is desperate, when all other help is vain, and what do you find? A door slammed in your face.... After that, silence."[4]

Jerry Boykin collapsed in grief and tears as the pressure of that terrible day in Mogadishu let up and the full reality of what had happened began to sink in. "I got angry," he said. "My chest was heaving. The more I cried, the more angry I got. Finally, I said, 'There is no God. If so, he would have prevented this. He would have heard my prayers.' And then, for the second time in my life, I really heard the voice of God: He said, *If there's no God, there's no hope.* Think about that: there's no hope for anything. I said, 'Lord, I'm sorry I doubted you, but where are you? Why'd you let this happen?' I picked up my Bible and opened it to Proverbs 3:5. 'Trust in the LORD with all your heart and lean not on your own understanding.' It was as if God was saying, *You can't understand. Just trust me.*"

JOB'S LESSONS ON LOSS

When it comes to facing the hard issues of grief and loss, there is no better example than that of Job. Even though he had lost his family, possessions, and eventually his health, he realized that everything he had before had been given to him by God. So God had the right to take it away. We should hold things with an open hand; when they're taken, we won't feel as if they've been torn from us. This hard-learned lesson allowed Job to make this ultimate statement of trust: "Though he slay me, yet will I hope in him" (Job 13:15).

One thing we must not do, in an effort to try to mitigate a person's grief, is to treat death as anything other than what it is: a tragedy, a black stain, a violation of the created order as God intended it. Death is a stench in God's nostrils. In the story about Jesus and Lazarus in John 11, we read that Jesus was "deeply moved in spirit and troubled" (v. 33). In the original Greek, the first of these terms ("deeply moved in spirit") connotes anger. Jesus was mad about the unjust ravages that death had visited upon his creation. The next word ("troubled") expresses agitation. Lazarus had been a beloved friend, and Jesus shared in the common feeling of grief over his death. Overcome by emotion, Jesus burst into tears (see John 11:35).

I don't know how many times I've heard someone say, "Death is part of life." *No!* I want to scream. *Death is DEATH!* Again, Lewis has a keen insight on this:

> But here is something quite different. Here is something telling me—well, what? Telling me that I must never, like the Stoics, say that death does not matter. Nothing is less Christian than that. Death which made Life Himself shed tears at the grave of Lazarus, and shed tears of blood in Gethsemane. This is an appalling horror; a stinking indignity. (You remember Thomas Browne's splendid remark: "I am not so much afraid of death, as ashamed of it.")[5]

Staff Sergeant Toph Bailey of the Oregon National Guard understands this, even if he didn't describe it quite as elegantly as Lewis. After describing the horrible injuries and deaths he had witnessed in Iraq, he said, "I couldn't stand the thought of my body being that torn and deformed. It would almost have been embarrassing for me if people saw me that contorted, misshaped, and exposed. While a dead soldier's memory is honored, his body has lost all dignity. That is what I feared."

He also touched on an important truth to help us through grieving: the importance of memorials. A tragic mistake the military made in Vietnam was not formalizing opportunities for soldiers to mourn their fallen comrades. Indeed, the personnel policy during that war, in which men were rotated into and out of units as individuals and not as a group, contributed to much of the soldiers' psychological harm. A soldier or Marine could see a friend killed in a rice paddy one night and within forty-eight hours he would be landing at San Francisco airport, DEROS'ed back to the States right on schedule. (DEROS stood for date of estimated return from overseas. The military bureaucracy is nothing if not efficient.) He had no time to mourn his buddy's death. Throw in the culture shock of suddenly being back in "The World," out of danger and with virtually no time to decompress, and you've set the grieving soldier up for some tough times.

Today's military better understands the dynamics of unit cohesion; soldiers rotate into and out of a war zone as units, not as individuals. Men and women who have lived and trained together for months or years naturally make a much better fighting force. The morale and trust factor also is much higher. Accordingly, a loss can hit the soldiers much harder. But that is why it is much more common to see formal memorial services for the fallen, both in the combat zone and upon return to a home base in the States. It gives warriors an opportunity to talk through their grief. It helps them to again feel close to a lost comrade.

Jonathan Shay, author of the books *Achilles in Vietnam* and *Odysseus in America* and a psychologist specializing in the treatment of post-traumatic stress disorder in Vietnam veterans, offers useful tips on effective grieving. For instance, a memorial service, as with any military ceremony, is going to have a senior officer speaking at some point. But it's also important to let a dead soldier's closest friends speak or pray, too, regardless of their rank. As Shay points out, "The 'hierarchy of bereavement,' that is, the ranking of intensity of attachment to the dead, rarely coincides with hierarchy or rank or military occupational specialty."[6]

Most important, a memorial allows us to offer God's comfort to one another: "The LORD is close to the brokenhearted and saves those who are crushed in spirit" (Psalm 34:18). And in offering comfort, we have to be careful not to resort to platitudes: *Well, he's in heaven now. It's for the better.* Such sentiments do nothing to ease the bereaved person's feelings of pain and loss.

You can cite an often-misused passage of Scripture, Romans 8:28 ("And we know that in all things God works for the good of those who love him, who have been called according to his purpose"), but do so *correctly,* not leaving off the portion of the verse that makes clear that this ultimate hope is for those who love God and trust him. Realize, also, that some questions have no answers. It's more important to simply *listen* to the grieving person than to offer pat answers.

Finally, remember that comforting is God's job. We are just the tools he uses. The late Dr. B. Clayton Bell, former pastor of Highland Park Presbyterian Church in Dallas, notes:

> God alone is the God of all comfort. He is the source; we are the channels. A competent physician knows how to clean a wound, apply antiseptic, suture where necessary, bandage, and then wait for the natural healing process. A doctor is not a healer. He aids the healing process that God controls and has built into the forces of nature. A good doctor knows his limitations and has the patience to wait for "nature" to heal. The same is true with the wounds of grief. God is the healer and fellow Christians can mediate his comfort. Yet, they also must know how to keep their hands off to allow God to do his own healing.[7]

Finally, a memorial service can provide an opportunity to offer the grieving a chance to understand the ultimate hope we have in Jesus. (More on this in the next chapter.) Jesus rose from the dead. He promised that we could live with him forever (see John 14:2–3). He told his friends, "I am the resurrection and the life. He who believes in me will live, even though he dies; and whoever lives and believes in me will never die" (John 11:25–26).

Grief is not the end. There is a way out of it, though it takes time. C. S. Lewis poignantly wrote, "I thought I could make a map of sorrow. Sorrow, however, turns out to be not a state but a process. It needs not a map but a history. Grief is like a long valley, a winding valley where any bend may reveal a totally new landscape."[8]

And, eventually, a way out.

★★★★

Life Practices That
Alleviate the Burden of Grief

Hopefully, you will never have to carry the burden of grief that Lieutenant General Jerry Boykin bore in Mogadishu. But if you serve in a war zone, chances are good that during your tour of duty you will witness injury and death, and you might lose a close friend. Grief is a hard reality of military life, so it's good to have practical steps you can take to address your grief.

1. Ask God for his comfort. In Matthew 5:4, Jesus says those who mourn are "blessed," because they will receive comfort. In 2 Corinthians 1:3, Paul describes the Lord as "the Father of compassion and the God of all comfort." Take God at his word and ask him to come and be your Comforter.

2. Seek the presence of God's Spirit. When the disciples were troubled at the thought that Jesus would be leaving them, Jesus comforted them by explaining that he would not leave them alone, but that his Father would send the Holy Spirit to be with them (see John 14:16–17, 26–27). The Holy Spirit is with you now. Don't fail to seek his power in the midst of your grief.

3. Don't expect grief to pass too quickly. There is nothing wrong with you if your grief stays with you for weeks or even months. If you lost someone especially close to you, it will take a long time to process the loss. It is not a sign of weakness to continue to struggle with grief. But keep in mind that over time, God will heal the pain of your loss.

4. Recognize that grief might show up in other emotions. Don't be surprised if your grief produces anger, distraction, loneliness, impatience, even confusion. The death of a friend leaves a hole that can't be filled completely; it's a permanent change in your life. Such a loss will give rise to a variety of emotions, in addition to sadness.

5. Don't hesitate to question God. It's likely that much of your anger and confusion is directed toward God. Why did he allow such a tragedy to happen? Why didn't he protect your friend(s)? Why does he allow good men and women to die when evildoers survive and even thrive? King David asked the same question in ancient times, wondering why the evil prosper when the righteous continue to suffer (see Psalm 73:1–14). Just as David was bold in voicing his questions and confusion, don't hesitate to open up to God. Let him know about your anger, your doubt, your hardest questions. You can be honest with God; he won't mind.

6. No matter how dark things seem right now, claim the

promise of God. In the book of Jeremiah, God commits himself to continue to seek what is best for you: "'For I know the plans I have for you,' declares the Lord, 'plans to prosper you and not to harm you, plans to give you hope and a future'" (Jeremiah 29:11). Read that verse and claim it as your own.

7. Ask God to use you to comfort others. In 2 Corinthians 1:4, Paul wrote that believers are to comfort one another with the same comfort that they have received from God. Ask God to show you how you might offer support, a listening ear, or simply your presence with a friend who is grieving.

8. Ask God for the faith to trust him even in the face of loss. Job proclaimed what could very well be the ultimate statement of trust: "Though he slay me, yet will I hope in him" (Job 13:15). If you want, you can adapt the following statement of faith for your current period of grieving: "Even though what has happened makes no sense, and even though I feel like I am buried in sorrow, in spite of it all I will trust in God's love, his wisdom, and his good plans for me."

9. Meditate on the character of God. In Psalm 62:11–12, David described God's character using just two words: "strong" and "loving." It's essential that we trust in both of these attributes of God. He is always and forever good

and loving, which means he won't do anything that is to
our harm. At the same time, God is all-powerful; there is
nothing within his will that he cannot bring to pass. His
love means he won't do us harm; his strength means he
can perform anything for us that he wills.

10. Jesus understands your grief. Jesus himself, when he was
contemplating his execution as he prayed in the Garden of
Gethsemane, told his disciples: "My soul is overwhelmed
with sorrow to the point of death" (Matthew 26:38). He
fully understands the burden of your sorrow: "For we do
not have a high priest who is unable to sympathize with
our weaknesses, but we have one who has been tempted
in every way, just as we are—yet was without sin"
(Hebrews 4:15).

10

Finding God on the Frontline

There Is an Answer to the Question of Eternal Meaning

I am the light of the world.
Whoever follows me will never
walk in darkness.
—JESUS (JOHN 8:12)

Phil Downer shipped off to Vietnam in 1967 as a young
Marine machine-gunner. M-60 machine-gunners used to
joke about how short their life expectancy was in combat.
It was a perverse form of bravado. Because the M-60 had so much
firepower, it was target number one in any battle. Day after day
Downer watched as friends and comrades died around him.

After about six months, Downer was promoted to machine-gun
team leader, which meant he no longer had to carry the gun. That
task fell to the next man in the three-man team, John Atkinson Jr.,
a happy-go-lucky Marine who carried an adopted puppy in his flak
jacket. Downer's unit was sent on a company-sized ambush to the

Antenna Valley, near the Demilitarized Zone (DMZ). It was meant to be a surprise attack, and it was—except it was the Marines who were surprised. Viet Cong and North Vietnamese forces had turned the area into a death trap. Downer's company was pinned down in rice paddies and, within a minute, a third of the Marines had been killed or wounded. His platoon was sent to the left to try to relieve pressure on the main unit. As his machine-gun team made a turn on the trail, Downer was slammed to the ground by a tremendous force; at the same time, he felt a weight fall on his legs.

A sniper had unloaded an AK-47 at the machine-gun team. One bullet had hit Downer's pack, exploding cans of C rations but leaving Downer unharmed. The other bullets hit John Atkinson, who was dead before he hit the ground. He was twenty-two years old.

The sniper had let an entire squad pass, waiting to hit the machine-gunner. If the ambush had occurred three days earlier, Downer would have been the one carrying the M-60. "As absorbed as I was with the death of another friend, I came to a startling realization," he says. "John had taken my place in death."[1]

Eventually, Everyone Will Die

Those serving in the military are faced with life-and-death situations, and make life-and-death decisions, much more often than those in civilian life. It's understandable that the risks involved in military life would keep the matter of survival in the front of your mind. Answering the call of duty puts you in harm's way, and you accept that as part of your service to your country.

In the previous chapters, I have written in a way that assumes you are already a Christian. But what does it really mean to be a Christian? Let me begin to answer by first saying what it's *not*. Being a Christian is not about going to church, behaving in a certain way, or conforming to a list of dos and don'ts. Neither is it dependent on practicing a list of spiritual disciplines—prayer, reading the Bible, fasting, performing acts of charity, or giving money to a church. Sure, certain behaviors are expected of a Christian, but the way you act is not what makes you a Christian.

Neither is it possible to be "righteous enough" to earn a place in God's family. In fact, that's probably the most common misperception of what it takes to become a child of God. It's what Phil Downer believed the day his unit was ambushed in Vietnam. After Atkinson was killed, the Marines remained engaged in battle into the night. With Downer and his men taking fire from all sides, he bargained with God: *If you get me out of this, I'll do anything. I'll make something out of my life. I'll join a church.*

And God got him out of it—not only that battle, but out of the war. With his tour finished, Downer returned home. He went to college and law school, where he met his wife, Susy, before going on to become a successful trial attorney.

But life was empty. "We had lucrative professional careers and all the stuff the TV commercials told us we needed," he says. Their marriage was tense, at best, and Downer had an explosive temper. But he did carry through on one promise he had made to God: he joined a church, although the decision was based more on the church's architecture than its theology.

Over time he came to realize that being right with God did not depend on being religious. At a business luncheon, the speaker talked about how God was the driving force in his life.

"It was the first time I had ever heard anyone other than a clergyman speak with conviction about God," Downer remembers. "He was speaking from his heart about someone he knew personally and intimately. But the strongest impression was that despite his own business pressures and responsibilities, he communicated a sense of peace I could not even imagine."

Downer began reading the Bible, and one verse stood out: "But God demonstrates his own love for us in this: While we were still sinners, Christ died for us" (Romans 5:8). Just as John Atkinson had died in Downer's place in Vietnam, he now realized that Jesus had also died in his place.[2] But Jesus did not just die. He rose again on the third day. His death paid the penalty for the sins of mankind, and his resurrection was, in a way, the death-blow to death.

What Is a Christian?

If being a Christian is not dependent on how good you are or what religious activities you are involved in, then what is it? To be a Christian is to believe that Jesus Christ paid the penalty for your sins—*all* of your sins. But why can't we pay for our own sins through good deeds? Here's an analogy that helps explain why we can't.

Like many air bases around the country, Peterson Air Force Base in Colorado Springs, Colorado, provides a mock-up of a large passenger airplane so that firefighters can practice not only putting out the flames but also entering the burning craft to rescue passengers and crew. The firefighters stand next to the hulk of the aircraft, their hoses at the ready, as the plane's jet fuel explodes into roiling balls of orange-black flame. A blast of heat hits them, and the violent upward rushing of superheated air results in a fire tornado, a vortex of flame dancing atop the plane and twisting nearly fifty feet into the air. (Peterson shares a runway with the Colorado Springs airport, and I often wonder what civilian airline passengers think when they see a burning airplane-shaped object at the end of their runway!)

Wearing their firefighter's "silvers"—the suits are named for their metallic appearance—the men lean forward to anticipate the sudden surge of pressure from their fire hoses. The blast of water comes, and they wade into the fire, pushing the flames ahead of them with the water. Their first task is to blaze a path (no pun intended) to the interior of the plane to rescue "survivors." The jet fuel is real, and it burns as hot as a thousand degrees. Their silvers are these firefighters' most important piece of equipment. Without the suits, made from materials that protect them from the flames and reflect the heat away from their bodies, they would never get past the first blast of heat. As it is, the temperature inside the suits can reach nearly two hundred degrees, and a few firefighters have suffered minor burns from their sweat turning to steam inside the outfits.

But that's nothing compared to what the fire will do if it can find the slightest gap in their protection. Firefighters have suffered severe burns on the thinnest sliver of flesh exposed because of a carelessly applied glove or an improperly sealed boot. They must be completely covered or they can be badly burned—or even killed.

There is an important theological truth hidden in what these men do. How many times have you heard someone claim that he'll make it to heaven because, while he might sin a little, he's really no worse than anyone else? (If you think about it, it's interesting that people compare themselves to real lowlifes—Hitler and Stalin, say—but never to Mother Teresa or, their real example, Jesus Christ.

But it's pointless to compare yourself with anyone—lowlife or saint—because God doesn't grade on a curve. People seem to think that because they feel they have more "good" deeds than bad, that fact somehow will tip the scale in their favor. Not so. Jesus tells us, "Be perfect, therefore, as your heavenly Father is perfect" (Matthew 5:48). The standard is not "good enough" or "better than the next guy." It's perfection.

That's because God is holy. It's part of his essence, his nature. (You've heard that God can do anything, and in a sense that's true. But there is one thing even God can't do—change his nature. If he did, he would no longer be God.) His holiness is difficult for us to comprehend because, as sinners, we are so far from it. And as fire can't help but burn every unprotected thing it touches, God's holiness cannot help but destroy everything unholy that comes into his presence. First Samuel 6:20 says, "Who can stand in the presence of the LORD, this holy God?" Or try Isaiah 6:5, where the prophet gets but a glimpse of the absolute holiness of God, and his reaction is utter terror. "Woe to me!" he cries. "I am ruined." (I like the wording of this passage in the King James Version: "I am undone." This rendition comes from the Hebrew word *damah*: "to cease to be" or "to be destroyed.")

Perfection is the standard. But, if we're honest with ourselves, we know that's an impossible standard to meet. If we have to be perfect, then we don't stand a chance. Even a single sin is like the crack of exposed skin in the firefighter's protective suit; one thin sliver will kill you. Nothing we do, no good works, can protect us from the burning flame of God's holiness. Imagine putting on your rattiest set of clothes to go fight an aircraft fire. That's kind of what Isaiah had in mind when he wrote, "All our righteous acts are like filthy rags; we all shrivel up like a leaf, and like the wind our sins sweep us away" (Isaiah 64:6).

But things are not as hopeless as they might sound. You have something to protect you from the fire of God's holiness. As the firefighters are made fireproof by their suits, you can be made "holy-proof," protected from the burning holiness of God, which destroys all unholy things. Your silver suit is Jesus Christ himself. The apostle Paul writes, "You are all sons of God through faith in Christ Jesus, for all of you who were baptized into Christ have *clothed* yourselves with Christ" (Galatians 3:26–27). Christ wraps us in his holiness, and when we come into the presence of a holy God we are protected from the punishment our sins deserve. When God looks at us he doesn't see a sinful rebel; he sees his sinless Son who died for our sins and then rose from the dead.

Jesus' Sacrifice for You

This also gives you some idea of what happened on the cross. The apostle Paul writes, "God made him [Jesus] who had no sin to be sin for us, so that in him we might become the righteousness of God" (2 Corinthians 5:21). Jesus, in his crucifixion, exposed himself to the fiery heat of God's holiness and justice to take the punishment for you and me. Now that's incredible love.

But simply knowing this won't do you any good. It's like knowing all about the only medical treatment that will save your life from a deadly infection, but then failing to go ahead and take the treatment. You might listen to a presentation about the benefits of this treatment, read about it, study the details of why the treatment is effective, but still die from the infection. To be healed and protected from death, you have to commit yourself. You have to receive the treatment.

It's the same way with Christ's sacrifice for the deadly infection of sin. You have to *trust* Christ and what he accomplished by his death and resurrection. The Air Force firefighters have intellectual knowledge that their suits will protect them, but it takes faith to put on the silver suit and then step into the flames. Until you put all your trust in the truth that the Bible teaches, it's just head knowledge—interesting information, even inspiring, but lacking the power to heal you of the sin that is guaranteed to kill you. Until you put on Jesus, the only protective suit against God's burning holiness, you're not protected.

The Choice Is Yours

Don't put off this decision. No one is promised his next breath, much less another day of life. Navy chaplain Captain Larry Ellis gives a good illustration. While stationed with a Marine unit aboard the USS *Tarawa*, an amphibious assault ship, he had developed a relationship with a lance corporal. The young Marine had a lot to look forward to in life, so when Ellis talked to him about his need for a Savior, the Marine didn't see it as an urgent matter. He was basically a good guy; he was young, strong, handsome, and smart. "I'll decide later," the Marine repeatedly told the chaplain. They had several port calls coming up, and the lance corporal wanted to be able to partake of the pleasures those places afforded.

A few days later, Ellis was on Vulture's Row, the part of a ship's superstructure that overlooks the flight deck. (The military has a talent for morbid humor.) A CH-46 Sea Knight helicopter loaded with Marines was taking off. The usual practice is for the chopper to lift a few feet above the deck and then slip sideways to port until it is over water before going on its way. Just as this bird got over the water, however, a loud bang and cloud of smoke erupted from one of the engines. The chopper dropped, but through heroic flying the pilots caught control of the craft just before it hit the sea. And even though one engine was tearing itself apart, they managed to wrestle the bird back up and over the flight deck before finally losing control. It crashed onto the deck, shaking itself apart. The whirling rotor blades struck the deck and shattered, tearing into the fuselage and spraying the flight deck with shards of fiberglass. Miraculously, the only injuries were bangs and bruises.

Guess who was on that chopper. "That young lance corporal ran, not walked, to my office," Ellis said, laughing.

That day, the Marine received another chance. Who knows if it was his second chance or his millionth? Scripture says: "The Lord is not slow in keeping his promise, as some understand slowness. He is patient with you, not wanting anyone to perish, but everyone to come to repentance" (2 Peter 3:9). God is patient, but you don't know how many chances you have left, and it's foolish to live as if you deserve more leniency from God.

Under fire in an ambush in Vietnam, Phil Downer realized that machine-gunner John Atkinson had died in his place. The death of a fellow Marine made it possible for Downer to return home, get married, and start a family. But it didn't make it possible for him to join God's family and to be assured that he would live in eternity, in the presence of God. Only the death of Christ, the one perfect life that was sacrificed to pay for the sins of undeserving sinners, could save Downer from the judgment required by the holiness of God.

It's the same for you and me. We can't earn God's favor. Nothing we do will put us in his good graces. Only by trusting in the sacrifice of the one perfect Man, Jesus Christ, can we accept the coat of holiness given to us by the Son of God.

We all need a Savior. "Righteousness from God comes through faith in Jesus Christ to all who believe. There is no difference, for all have sinned and fall short of the glory of God, and are justified freely by his grace through the redemption that came by Christ Jesus" (Romans 3:22–24).

Jesus invites you to trust him: "If you confess with your mouth, 'Jesus is Lord,' and believe in your heart that God raised him from the dead, you will be saved" (Romans 10:9).

Any time is the right time to make the right decision. But why put it off?

★★★★

Life Practices That Call God Close

God is near at all times, but he is real only to those who have put their full trust in him. Here are a few ways you can seek God out and things you can do to find answers to your questions.

1. If you're not sure what to do, keep seeking God. Perhaps you have more questions and you need additional answers before you can fully trust God. If that's the case, take God at his word. He promises that if you seek him with "all your heart" you will find him (see Jeremiah 29:13). Don't rest until you have obtained the answers to your questions. Trust God to reveal himself to you as you honestly seek him.

2. Open up with God. The one Person in the universe who understands you completely is God. It's no surprise to him that you have doubts, or bitterness, or confusion. Tell him exactly what is on your heart and ask him to answer your doubts and clear up your confusion.

3. Read strategic passages of Scripture for insight, understanding, and direction. Here are a few to get you started: Romans 3:23; 5:7–8; 6:23; 2 Corinthians

5:21; Galatians 3:26–27; Ephesians 2:7–10; John 3:16.

4. Ask God to draw near and to open up your understanding. Understanding the gospel that Jesus died to pay the penalty for your sins and rose from the dead so you can live with him in eternity is a necessary first step. But to make it personal you need to commit yourself to God in faith. And for most of us, that's a scary step to take. So ask God to reveal himself to you so that you will sense his presence with you. Ask God to open the eyes of your spirit, so you can trust what is invisible and beyond mere intellectual understanding.

5. Ask God to help you overcome your doubts. A man asked Jesus to heal his son, and even as he asked he realized how weak his faith was. So the man did a wise thing: he confessed that he did believe in Jesus' power, and then he asked Jesus to help him believe more fully. The man's statement of faith is a prayer you can pray for yourself: "I do believe; help me overcome my unbelief" (Mark 9:24).

6. Faith is a gift, which means you can't earn it. Another way to think of faith is that it is a free gift that God hands to you. All you can do is hold out your hands and receive it; it's not a virtue that you can manufacture on your own. "For it is by grace you have been saved, through faith— and this not from yourselves, *it is the gift of God*" (Ephesians 2:8). "For it is God who works in you to will and

to act according to his good purpose" (Philippians 2:13). If you are struggling with trusting God, ask him to help you believe in him.

7. Don't put it off. No one knows better than the men and women in the military that none of us is guaranteed another day on earth. Life is fragile, so don't put off making a commitment to Christ. If you know the truth about his death and resurrection, then accept his forgiveness and the gift of eternal life. Don't put it off.

8. Ask for prayer. If you are still struggling, ask a Christian friend to pray for you. In fact, ask that friend to commit to pray for you regularly.

9. Ask a Christian chaplain for spiritual counsel. If questions are crowding your mind and keeping you from trusting God, ask a Christian chaplain to explain the biblical truth that will clear up your questions. Help is available, so take advantage of it.

Notes

Chapter 1

1. Chuck Holton, *A More Elite Soldier: Pursuing a Life of Purpose* (Sisters, Ore.: Multnomah Publishing, 2003), 15.
2. Augustine, *Confessions* (New York: Oxford University Press USA, reprint edition, 1998), 3.

Chapter 2

1. Edward V. Rickenbacker, "Seven Came Through," *Life,* January 25, 1943, p. 19–26.
2. Billy Graham, *Hope for Each Day* (Nashville, Tenn.: J. Countryman, 2002), 89.
3. As a young woman, Joni Eareckson Tada became a quadriplegic as a result of a diving accident, yet she has gone on to do great work for God as a speaker, writer, and artist. For more information visit www.joniandfriends.org.
4. Tom Neven, "Stealth Force," *Breakaway,* August 2002, 18–19. From the August 2002 *Breakaway* magazine.

5. Dietrich Bonhoeffer, "Prayers in Time of Distress," *Letters and Papers from Prison, The Enlarged Edition* (London: SCM Press, 1971). Reprinted with the permission of Scribner, an imprint of Simon & Schuster Adult Publishing Group, from *Letters and Papers from Prison, Revised, Enlarged Ed.* By Dietrich Bonhoeffer, translated from the German by R. H. Fuller, Frank Clark, al. Copyright © 1953, © 1967, ©1971 by SCM Press Ltd. All rights reserved.

Chapter 3

1. Archibald D. Hart, *Unmasking Male Depression* (Nashville, Tenn.: Word Publishing, 2001), 3.
2. National Institute of Mental Health, NIH Publication No. 00–3561, May 22, 2002.
3. University of Cincinnati Psychological Services Center. Found at http://www.uc.edu/psc/Depression_in_men.html (accessed on June 23, 2006).
4. Hart, *Unmasking Male Depression*, 46.
5. C. S. Lewis, *The Problem of Pain* (San Francisco, Calif.: HarperSanFrancisco, 2001), 161.
6. Lewis B. Puller Jr., *Fortunate Son: The Healing of a Vietnam Vet* (New York: Grove Weidenfeld, 1991), 158.
7. Dave Dravecky with Mike Yorkey, *Called Up: Stories of Life*

and Faith from the Great Game of Baseball (Grand Rapids, Mich.: Zondervan, 2004), 16–18.

8. Charles Haddon Spurgeon, *From the Metropolitan Tabernacle Pulpit* (London: Passmore and Alabaster, 1881), vol. 27, 1595.

9. Lewis, *The Problem of Pain*, 91.

10. Tom Neven, "Rescue at Sea," *Breakaway,* September 1999, 8. From the September 1999 *Breakaway* magazine. Copyright © 1999, Focus on the Family. All rights reserved. International copyright secured. Used by permission.

11. Lewis, *The Problem of Pain*, 91.

12. Fyodor Dostoyevsky, *The House of the Dead or Prison Life in Siberia* (Whitefish, MT: Kessinger Publishing, 2004), p. 25.

Chapter 4

1. *The 300 Spartans,* produced and directed by Rudolph Maté, screenplay by George St. George, Twentieth Century Fox, 1962.

2. Herodotus, *The Histories,* trans. Robin Waterfield (New York: Oxford University Press, USA; new ed edition, 1998), 484.

3. John S. D. Eisenhower, *The Bitter Woods: The Battle of the Bulge* (Cambridge, Mass.: Da Capo Press, 1995), 323. Among the units under McAuliffe's command was Easy Company of the 506th Regiment, 101st Airborne Division, the soldiers profiled in Stephen Ambrose's moving history *Band of Brothers.* That title is significant, taken as it is from

Shakespeare's *Henry V*, which gives an account of the incredible victory at Agincourt in October 1415, where the English army, outnumbered by a factor of as much as six to one, defeated a heavily armored French army on Saint Crispin's Day. Rallying his troops before the battle, King Hal, as he was known, gave what many consider the ultimate appeal to the brotherhood of soldiers:

> *This story shall the good man teach his son,…*
> *From this day to the ending of the world,*
> *But we in it shall be remember'd—*
> *We few, we happy few, we band of brothers;*
> *For he today that sheds his blood with me*
> *Shall be my brother; be he ne'er so vile,*
> *This day shall gentle his condition;*
> *And gentlemen in England now abed*
> *Shall think themselves accursed they were not here,*
> *And hold their manhoods cheap whiles any speaks*
> *That fought with us upon Saint Crispin's day*

(King Hal's speech taken from William Shakespeare, *Henry V,* Folger Shakespeare Library Edition [New York: Washington Square Press, 2004], 165.)

4. "FBI probes military-gang ties," by Charles Sheehan, *Chicago*

Tribune, May 2, 2006. "Gangs claim their turf in Iraq," by Frank Main, *Chicago Sun-Times,* May 1, 2006.

Chapter 5

1. *Sands of Iwo Jima,* directed by Allan Dwan, produced by Edmund Grainger, screenplay by James Edward Grant and Harry Brown, Republic Pictures, 1949.
2. Joe Louis, cited in Ellie Kay, *The Debt Diet* (Minneapolis, Minn.: Bethany House, 2005), 41. Also cited in Lloyd Cory, *Quote Unquote* (Wheaton, Ill.: Victor Books, 1977), 88. Also cited in J. Lyman MacInnis, *Life Is Like a Taxi Ride* (London: Harper Collins Ltd., 1997).

Chapter 6

1. W. Cates Jr., "Estimates of the Incidence and Prevalence of Sexually Transmitted Diseases in the United States," American Social Health Association Panel, *Sexually Transmitted Diseases,* 1999; 26 (Supp): 2–7; and H. Weinstock, S. Berman, and W. Cates, "Sexually Transmitted Diseases Among American Youth: Incidence and Prevalence Estimates, 2000," *Perspectives on Sexual and Reproductive Health,* 2004; 36(1):6–10.
2. Ramona Richards, "Dirty Little Secret." www.christianitytoday .com/tcw/2003/005/5.58.html (accessed on March 6, 2006).
3. Susan Dominus, "What Women Want to Watch," *The New York Times,* August 29, 2004.

4. Mark O'Keefe, "Women Account for Hefty Portion of Web Porn Viewing," Newhouse News Service. www.newhouse.com/ archive/okeefe103103.html (accessed on March 6, 2006).
5. "Is the Internet Bad for Your Marriage? Online Affairs, Pornographic Sites Playing Greater Role in Divorces," PR Newswire, 14 November 2002.
6. Victor B. Cline, *Pornography's Effects on Adults & Children* (New York: Morality in Media, 1999), 5.
7. Testimony of Dr. Judith Reisman, "The Science Behind Pornography Addiction," U.S. Senate Committee on Commerce, Science and Transportation Web site, (expert witness testimony). http://commerce.senate.gov/hearings/witnesslist.cfm?id=1343 (accessed on March 6, 2006).
8. Testimony by Daniel Weiss, senior analyst for media and sexuality, Focus on the Family, at the May 19, 2005, Summit on Pornography: Obscenity Enforcement, Corporate Participation and Violence against Women and Children. Found at http://www.family.org/cforum/fosi/pornography/ljaei/a0036586.cfm. Accessed on June 24, 2006.
9. C. S. Lewis, *Mere Christianity* (San Francisco, Calif.: HarperSanFrancisco, Harper Edition 2001), 95.

Chapter 7
1. Greg Jaffe, "For Army Families, Repeat Tours Strain Life on

Home Front," *The Wall Street Journal,* December 16, 2005.

2. Donna Mills, "Army Divorce Rates Drop as Marriage Programs Gain Momentum," American Forces Press Service, January 27, 2006.

3. Jaffe, "For Army Families, Repeat Tours Strain Life on Home Front," 1.

4. Edna J. Hunter, *Families Under the Flag* (New York: Praeger Publishing, 1982), 24.

5. You can read about this in the excellent book *Flags of Our Fathers,* by James Bradley with Ron Powers (New York: Bantam, 2000).

6. Michael E. Ruane, "A Union Tested by War," *The Washington Post,* March 28, 2006.

7. Jay MacInnes, "Battle Scars: Dave Roever Shares the Pain and Purpose," *Lifewise,* April/May 2003. www.family.org/focusoverfifty/lifewise/a0026233.cfm./ (accessed on April 20, 2006). Used by permission of the author. All rights reserved. To learn more about Dave Roever and his ministry to young people, visit www.daveroever.net.

Chapter 8

1. Gordon W. Prange, *God's Samurai* (Dulles, Va.: Potomac Books, 2003), 34–35.

2. Adapted from *Finding Forgiveness at Pearl Harbor* by Jacob DeShazer, copyright © Cook Communications Ministries

International, 4050 Lee Vance View, Colorado Springs, CO 80918 USA. Used by permission.

3. Homer, *The Iliad*, public domain. The quote is taken from the Gutenberg Project's English translation of *The Iliad*. Found at www.gutenberg.org/etext/2199./ (accessed on June 25, 2006).

4. Homer, *The Iliad*.

5. Homer, *The Iliad*.

6. Quoted in Jonathan Shay, M.D., PhD, *Achilles in Vietnam* (New York: Antheneum, 1994), 78–79.

7. DeShazer, *Finding Forgiveness at Pearl Harbor*.

8. DeShazer, *Finding Forgiveness at Pearl Harbor*.

Chapter 9

1. C. S. Lewis, *A Grief Observed* (San Francisco, Calif.: Harper-SanFrancisco, 2001), 3.

2. Homer, *The Iliad*, public domain. The quote is taken from the Gutenberg Project's English translation of *The Iliad*. www.gutenberg.org/etext/2199./ (accessed on June 25, 2006).

3. Jonathan Shay, M.D., PhD, *Achilles in Vietnam* (New York: Antheneum, 1994), 63.

4. Lewis, *A Grief Observed*, 5.

5. C. S. Lewis, *God in the Dock: Essays on Theology and Ethics* (Grand Rapids, Mich.: Wm. B. Eerdmans; Reprint edition, 1994), 86–87.

6. Shay, *Achilles in Vietnam,* 199.

7. Peggy and Clayton Bell, "A Look at Grief," *Leadership,* October 1, 1980, www.ctlibrary.com/12879.

8. Lewis, *A Grief Observed,* 59.

Chapter 10

1. Phil Downer, quoted by Tom Neven, "From Hell to Eternity," *Focus on the Family,* November 2002, 12–13. From the November 2002 *Focus on the Family* magazine. Copyright © 2002, Focus on the Family. All rights reserved. International copyright secured. Used by permission.

2. Downer, quoted by Tom Neven, "From Hell to Eternity."

About the Author

From an early age, Tom Neven has wanted to be only two things in life: a Marine and a writer. He joined the Marine Corps upon graduating from high school and went on to serve seven years as an M-60 machine-gunner and an embassy guard in Africa and Europe. After being honorably discharged, he earned a bachelor's degree in philosophy, graduating *magna cum laude* from Wheaton College in Illinois, and then attended the Columbia University Graduate School of Journalism.

His writing has been published in a number of periodicals, including the *Washington Post,* the *Denver Post,* the *Rocky Mountain News,* and *Writer's Digest.* He covered the first Gulf War for the *Marine Corps Gazette* and went on to serve as editor of *Focus on the Family* magazine for six years. In the course of his journalism career he has joined the 9G club while flying an F-16 fighter, landed on an aircraft carrier (the USS *Abraham Lincoln*), driven a Bradley Fighting Vehicle, and spent three days submerged in a Navy attack submarine (the USS *Pasadena*). He also is an avid scuba diver and skier.

Neven has been married twenty-five years to Colette, whom he met and married while he was an embassy guard in Geneva, Switzerland. They have two children, Joshua and Hannah.

To learn more about WaterBrook Press and view
our catalog of products, log on to our Web site:
www.waterbrookpress.com

WATERBROOK
PRESS